One Shepherd,

OLIVER BARRES

One Shepherd,
One Flock

CATHOLIC ANSWERS
SAN DIEGO
2000

Unless otherwise noted, Scripture quotations are taken from the *Revised Standard Version Catholic Edition* (RSVCE) © 1946–1966, Division of Christian Education of the National Council of the Churches of Christ in the United States of America.

Published by Catholic Answers, Inc.
2020 Gillespie Way
El Cajon, California 92020
(888) 291-8000 (orders)
(619) 387-0042 (fax)
www.catholic.com (web)
Cover design by Laurie Miller

Printed in the United States of America
ISBN 1–888992–19–0

Contents

PART ONE: THRESHOLD THOUGHTS

PART TWO: CATHOLICISM OR CHAOS

For our grandchildren
here and yet to come

Nathaniel Barres Cotter
Laura Margaret Cawthon
John Oliver Cotter
Diana Elizabeth Riggs
Paul Barry Cotter III
William Clark Cawthon
Michael Barres Cawthon
Thomas Richard Gill
Jonathan Grandon Gill
Katherine Ann Barres

Preface

This book is a classic in the art of apologetics, the art of defending and explaining the Catholic faith. It is happily reprinted now when apologetics is coming back into importance, having been eclipsed for some decades by the age of ecumenism. The creation of a more Christian climate of dialogue and cooperation between the churches was an important contribution of Vatican II, and apologetics, an ancient art, was less emphasized at least by Catholics and main line Protestants. Now Catholic laymen, even lay theologians, many of whom have been Evangelicals, have put a whole new emphasis on apologetics.

Oliver Barres' account of the journey he and his wife, both Congregational ministers, made to the Church founded by Christ, not only brings back a great age of converts, but puts a fresh light on the essential issues. Frank Sheed, that legendary apologist of the past, describes Oliver Barres as having a hunger and thirst for reality, "for the objective".

The hunger for truth has almost been lost in our society, which focuses much more on need fulfillment and personal satisfaction. We forget that there is a more substantial road which all too few recognize, the truth. Fr. Avery Dulles, S.J., himself a convert from about the same time, sees the republication of *One Shepherd, One Flock* as fitting well into the spiritual climate of our times. It speaks to the present-day converts and those who are searching, while Barres offers to all thinking Catholics an opportunity "to recover the past but also to discern the shape of the future."

Barres' afterword is especially interesting for those who read this book a half century ago. Like myself these readers will be delighted to learn that the struggles of the two ministerial "nomads" have led to a remarkably happy conclusion. While searching for Christ they also found the hundredfold of which he speaks.

Fr. Benedict J. Groeschel, C.F.R.

Foreword

I first had the pleasure of reading this book when it was published in 1956. About the same time, Oliver Barres wrote for *America* an article which so impressed me that I kept it in my files for more than thirty years.[1] In 1987, when the now Monsignor, John Barres became my student at The Catholic University of America, he asked me whether I had ever heard of his father. As proof that I had, I passed on to him the article just mentioned. I trust that it is still in his keeping as he enters upon his new position as Chancellor of the Diocese of Wilmington, Delaware.

Oliver Barres and his wife Marjorie are a remarkable couple. Married in 1946 in the chapel of Yale Divinity School where they were both students at the time, they were ordained in a joint ceremony on June 14, 1951. After four years of happy and successful ministry in the Congregational Church, they both embraced what they took to be the fullness of Christianity by becoming Catholics in 1955.

The Barreses were by no means alone in their journey. They were part of a significant wave of conversions to Roman Catholicism in the mid-twentieth century. Typically, the converts came from liberal Protestant or Anglican backgrounds but came to feel that their former churches had drifted away from the faith of the early centuries and had accommodated too much to modern culture. Catholicism had enormous attractive power because of its worldwide unity, its rich tradition, its vigorous sacramental life, its strong dogmatic faith, and its firm moral discipline. Characteristically, too, the converts welcomed the Catholic accent on rationality and truth. Many of the converts, through European

---

[1] The article was, I believe, "In Praise of Protestants," *America* 94 (January 21, 1956): 448-49.

travel, had gained some familiarity with the art, architecture, and piety of Catholic Europe.

I can speak with conviction of this movement because I was caught up in it. After having traveled considerably in Western Europe as a boy, I studied the civilization of the Middle Ages and the Renaissance as an undergraduate at Harvard. A few months after graduating from college, I was received into the Catholic Church in the fall of 1940, as a first-year student at Harvard Law School. In 1946 I published an account of my own journey of faith, and in 1996 reprinted it with an afterword, much as Oliver Barres has done with the present book.[2]

For all these reasons, the apologia of Oliver Barres speaks powerfully to me. Although he wrote a decade later than I, and with the benefit of a richer theological education, we were both motivated by a similar realization that modern-day subjectivism and individualism were leading to chaos and undermining the harmony of faith and reason that had brought Western civilization to such great heights.

As Frank Sheed points out in his introduction to the original edition, Oliver Barres was relentlessly rational. Driven by a pure passion for truth, he had every right to quote from an earlier convert, John Dryden, as he does in his afterword:

> For truth has such a face and such a mien,
> As to be loved needs only to be seen.

The great reward, of course, is truth itself, not as an abstract idea but as a living person who can dare to say of himself, "I am the truth." The prize of faith is the hidden treasure, the pearl of great price, for which the wise merchant will gladly sell all he possesses (Matt. 13:44–45).

In the case of the Barreses, the search was free from all self-interest. Indeed, they embraced truth at the price of considerable sacrifice, since it meant surrendering their careers as ordained min-

---

[2] *A Testimonial to Grace and Reflections on a Theological Journey* (Kansas City, Mo.: Sheed & Ward, 1996).

isters and becoming, for a while, "thirty-three-year-old mendicants," living on the hospitality of the Abbey of Regina Laudis in
Bethlehem, Connecticut. But God takes wonderful care of those
who seek his Kingdom above all else. Trusting in him, Oliver
and Marjorie found productive paths of service in their adopted
Church and raised six children, all of whom seem to have been
happy in their faith and successful in their respective walks of life.

There was a moment in the turbulent aftermath of the Second
Vatican Council when the value of books such as this might have
been questioned. Were they too assertive, too "triumphalist," too
authoritarian, too papist? Did not Vatican II recommend a more
collegial and diversified Church, a more democratic polity, greater
scope for dissent, and a more positive evaluation of non-Roman
Catholic Christianity?

During the decade between 1965 and 1975, Catholicism in certain places, including much of the English-speaking world, seemed
to be losing its nerve and seeking to minimize its most distinctive
features. Conversions slowed down to a trickle. But it now seems
fair to say that the true directions of the Council have been more
accurately assessed. Pope John Paul II has found a path through
the conflict of interpretations. Thanks to his wise and energetic
leadership, Catholic doctrine has regained its balance and clarity.
The Church is once more in a position to evangelize the modern
world. And the flow of conversions has resumed.

The republication of books such as this fits well into the present-
day spiritual climate. Conversion stories published in the past
decade have a great deal in common with that of Oliver Barres.
Look, for example, at the immensely popular account written
by Scott and Kimberly Hahn, a Presbyterian couple thoroughly
grounded in Reformation theology.[3] The logic of conversion is
still much the same. The insights that guided Oliver and Marjorie
Barres not only permit us to recover the past but also to discern
the shape of the future. Their story can help contemporary Cath-

---

[3] Scott and Kimberly Hahn, *Rome Sweet Home: Our Journey to Catholicism*
(San Francisco: Ignatius, 1993).

olics to appreciate what is abidingly valid in their own tradition —including allegedly problematic doctrines such as the Petrine office, infallibility, the real presence of Christ in the Eucharist, priestly orders, Mary and the saints, purgatory, and the auricular confession of sins. By showing how they came to believe in doctrines such as these, converts such as Oliver Barres can make a special contribution to authentic ecumenism and to the reinvigoration of Catholic Christianity. The truth of Catholic doctrine never grows old.

AVERY DULLES, S.J.
Fordham University
Bronx, New York

Introduction

By the mere chance of a speaking engagement in Hartford, I was the first Catholic to whom Oliver Barres talked of joining the Church. He was then a Congregational minister, his wife a Congregational minister too. With his conversion I had nothing whatever to do: he had thought or read or prayed his way through to every one of the conclusions of this book before we met. No one talked him into a single step of the way—there never was a more impersonal conversion, humanly speaking.

That goes with the basic quality of his mind. He has a hunger and thirst for reality, for the objective. That a creed stimulates or consoles or quiets the conscience, that it meets one's desires or felt needs—all that is splendid, but secondary. Unless it is true, he will have none of it. "Who," he cries, "looking into the deceitfulness of his own heart, can hope to cast anchor in subjectivity?" Subjectivity can run shallow or deep, as mere desire for peace of mind or as anguished search for "the continuity of the experiential note"; but, so long as man's reaction is the test, "truth falls by the wayside, a maimed, battered and broken wreck." Truth is not what appeals; truth is what *is*. Only reality nourishes.

Everyone sees the division of sects as a scandal, but where most see it as a clouding of love, Oliver Barres saw it also as a despair of truth. Despair is the precise word. It is not simply that the Christian churches are divided *now* as to what Christ meant; it is that the divisions cannot be healed ever. Even if they reunited, they could not stay agreed, for the same root principles—private judgment in the individual, a Church not seen as speaking with the authority of Christ—which caused the fissuring in the past, would still be there to start the fissuring process all over again.

If that is the whole story, then clearly truth must not matter—anyhow, it did not matter enough for Christ to provide for our getting it. That was the point Oliver Barres had reached when his diary opens. Either there is a voice here upon earth telling us Christ's meaning with Christ's authority, or we cannot know his meaning—we can but make our own choice among the thousand guesses of men. Since there was a voice upon earth claiming to be *that* Voice, he must see if its claim was true. He came at last to accept the Catholic Church, not from a weak man's need for authority but from a sane man's need for truth, which is reality known.

The diary, written to clarify his own mind but in the awareness that it might be needed to explain his action to others, covers the period from March to December 1954. By the end of it, he had no doubts left. But he did not resign his ministry till the following Easter: he must be certain of his certainty, sure that he was not casting anchor in subjectivity after all.

It would be a wonderful thing if Marjorie Barres had kept a diary, too. It would, I think, have been very different. She started later than her husband and moved along a different road. They were received into the Church together, their two small girls with them, on the Vigil of Pentecost. The day of their First Communion was Pentecost Day.

F. J. SHEED

PART ONE

THRESHOLD THOUGHTS

First Day of Spring   21 March 1954[1]

Strong stone walls surround the green pastureland of an Eastern sheepfold. There is but one small gate by which the sheep go in and out, and the watchful shepherd posts himself at this gate.

When first I heard the voice of the Roman shepherd, it sounded strange and repellent. The words were arrogant. The tone of command offended me. I looked at the gate, and it was too narrow for the passage of my possessions. Angrily I turned away.

I wandered through the heat of a lifeless desert, up the rocky crags of mountain wastelands, on and on past deep harrowed fields and sunless glens to the uttermost parts of the earth. But wherever I fled, the voice of that shepherd kept sounding in my ear, until at last I knew that I must return.

And so I have come back once again to the sheepfold and the narrow gate. Hesitant, uncertain, I stand now upon the threshold, thinking and looking in.

Turning and Returning   23 March 1954

I built a snowman for my daughter, and I gave him eyes of stone, and he was blind. When he melted away, I told her he had "turned to water." Now she turns on her toes like a miniature ballet dancer, pirouetting round and round, as she sings to herself, "Snowman turn—snowman turn to water."

Is thirty-two any wiser than two-and-a-half? A child with a false notion gets no dizzier than a man who sees the light, when the light that he sees turns out to be darkness.

The merciful God cries out: "Return, lost ones, return." Therefore, let us search and try our ways, and turn again to the Lord.

Old New England   31 March 1954

For the past month a semicircle of black crepe has bordered the farmer's field across from our rural Connecticut parsonage. But now as I look out the study window, I can see that the ground surge of spring has been steadily at work conquering the hard dead earth. The black semicircle has grown green, and the birds have returned.

The farmer in his New England reticence dislikes the unexpected intruder. He loves his predictable herd of brown-and-white Guernseys. His world is small, and he likes it that way.

One day last fall I angled across the field toward the long red barn. As he drove past astride an ancient horse-pulled mower, he was mumbling about getting the law after trespassers. I looked down into the viewer of my camera, managed the scattered cows and the big white church into pattern, then waited till the mower took its place.

"Click," said the camera.

"Humph," grunted the farmer.

"Moo," moaned the nervous herd, hastily shuffling away from the strange intruder.

About a month ago, on a windless afternoon, the elderly farmer and his friendly wife were out burning their field's black border. The weeds were thick, and the smoke billowed high. The farmer's wife in an old apron was trimming a vigorous forsythia bush by the roadside. At the edge of the field, a few feet away, her husband wielded the torch.

"Your field looks quite stately in that border of black crepe," I suggested. "Has your favorite field mouse died?"

He gave me a curt, cryptic nod and moved quickly away.

Easter in Italy   9 April 1954

My mind goes back ten years to the Holy Week of 1944. The priest's bedroom in the rectory was the safest spot in a mountain village called Vallerotonda. The protection of heavy church walls and two ceilings above made it practically certain that a Jerry 88 shell would not intrude. The ambulance driver I was relieving had discovered this hideaway. He recommended it highly— unless, that is, I happened to be a fire-eater of the boldest sort. Which I was not.

Outside in the rain the Tommies were milling silently about.

Their feet slushed through the oozing mud. Their hands busily packed the patient burros with heavy kit, ammo, hard tack, and bully beef, in preparation for a probing attack. About the village the olive groves were splintered and torn by mortar fire. The straw in the slit trenches was sodden wet. Maggots ate at the carcass of a dead horse. And there were fire-gutted vehicles on the edge of the narrow winding road.

At 11 P.M. one clear night, a fellow driver awoke me with a cry: "Two ambulances needed—let's go!" We followed a fast jeep over the hill to the place where they had brought the wounded men. A green young officer had taken them into a moonlit field to bed down, and of course Jerry had immediately shelled them.

The roads were pockmarked and bumpy. The stretcher cases cursed us as we negotiated our way through the rubble-strewn ghost town of Acquafondata to the Eighth Army's casualty clearing station at Casale.

Meanwhile, not far away, half-crazed rats and humans scurried through the ruins of the mother monastery of the Benedictine order. For throughout Holy Week great fleets of our American bombers were pounding the Germans in the abbey atop Monte Cassino, just a few miles west of us along the Gothic line.

Such was *l'Italia bellissima* on a bloody beastly Easter morning —9 April 1944.

Two months later the Gothic Line had fallen, Cassino had been bypassed, and our vehicles moved northward at last. Joyfully I set down this jingle in my Italian Journal:

> I live within my ambulance,
> A cozy little home
> Of blankets, bugs and bandages
> All rolling on to Rome!

Under Judgment   10 April 1954

Last Thursday in Hartford's Congregational "cathedral," after the weekly meeting of town and country clergy, I was the neutral party at a heated discussion between two fellow ministers. Here was an example of the difficulties we meet in trying to maintain a spirit of charity within Protestant disunity.

B.[2] is an African-American pastor in an interracial housing project. He is still in his twenties, a straightforward, earnest, clean-cut young fellow. He was saying that in his Easter sermon he planned to ask this question: "What sort of a world, and what kind of people, would put an innocent man to death on a cross?"

"This has nothing to do with my being a Negro," he added thoughtfully. "The problem goes deeper than that."

He spoke of God's wrath at seeing his Son rejected. He noted the easy conscience of modern man and his secret longing for the word of judgment.

That word *judgment* brought L. into the battle. He had spoken Monday evening at a Home Lenten Meeting in my parish, so I knew what to expect. His father had treated him harshly as a child. In reaction the son had left the Church of his youth and entered the ministry of another.

His own approach to parishioners is one of *acceptance*. "I love them under all conditions. 'You may be blustering, or ugly, or cruel,' I think, 'but I'm all for you just the same.' Show people the least sign of rejection or disapproval, and you never reach their hearts. Love is the only force that ever does any real good."

B. disagreed. "Don't use that word *love* any more," he urged. "It's sickly. People need honesty, not sentimentality. Unconsciously they long for judgment. They want to hear a voice objectifying their innermost guilts and frustrations. If you hate your neighbor, for heaven's sake admit it."

"That's how the Reformation started," I suggested. "Luther became honest enough to say, 'Love God? I hate him!' "

"That's it," the Negro boy agreed enthusiastically. "Honesty!"

Our warm-hearted friend began to attack the foolishness of this harsh approach. Liberalism would not stand for it. He shifted gears and gave a short appreciation of A. N. Whitehead. We had spoken of this scientific philosopher after the Home Lenten Meeting. Never having read his books, I had merely nodded my head sagaciously and let it go at that. But since then I have learned that Whitehead believes in a God who is organic with the world and in no sense transcendent. This is certainly not the God of Abraham, Isaac, and Jacob.

L. was talking about the need for revival and his desire to recapture the best of John Wesley. "Billy Graham is doing God's work all right, but he's trying to use outdated methods. Most of us will never get the opportunity God has given him. Look what he's doing in England! I pray for him every day, but I wish he'd study Wesley."

Here was a paradox indeed: a preacher who desired to imitate Wesley while denying that saint's basic premises. John Wesley was no vague and sentimental liberal. His evangelical enthusiasm used to full advantage the lever of judgment, echoing Christ's own words on eternal punishment. The saving of souls from the fires of hell was the great passion of early Methodism. Revival without that lever of truth may well be a worthy desire, but it is also a proven impossibility.

Twice a week I play volleyball at the Hartford YMCA. One of the boys, an insurance company arson investigator, recently gave me a copy of Arnold Lunn's *Now I See*, in which I came across this observation about Wesley and revival.

> Churches are vital in exact proportion to the number of Catholic doctrines which they retain. English nonconformity was lapsing into Arianism when Wesley launched his campaign, a campaign which owed its success to his insistence on Catholic doctrines, on the deity of Christ in the full Nicene sense of the term, on free will against the Calvinists, and on the Catholic doctrine of eternal punishment.[3]

I have also been reading Ronald Knox's study *Enthusiasm*, in which he calls Wesley "a cheerful experimentalist who in all the hesitations of a lifetime never asked himself by what right he ruled, or on what basis of intellectual certainty he believed."[4]

Now it is true, as I see it, that John Wesley fostered the religion of experience and thereby helped to lure our modern world into the swamplands of subjectivism. But he himself kept the faith.

He firmly maintained the objective truth of the basic Christian dogmas, among which was our Lord's teaching on eternal punishment.

But L. disliked the whole idea of judgment. Even the Negro minister agreed with him that the word *hell* should not be used in the pulpit. The only noise he disapproved of more vehemently was the mushy, maudlin sound of that word *love*.

They had been plumbing such theological depths for an hour when I asked them to join me in a short cooling-off prayer.

"Almighty God, our heavenly Father, mediate to each of us your love and your truth, that we may lose neither; through Jesus Christ our Lord. Amen."

As we walked out toward the busy city street, we passed the stained-glass windows of the gothic sanctuary. What an anomaly! Here in the heart of religious liberalism was a Congregational "cathedral" containing a luminous window for each apostle. How our Puritan ancestors would writhe at the sight! President Timothy Dwight of Yale, denouncing the celebration of our Lord's own birthday, had stated pontifically: "It is an heinous sin to celebrate Christ-mass." How he would glower and glare at the impertinence of the ornate gold cross within this popish sanctuary! And what would he think of the new window near the altar? The present "dean of the cathedral" had told me about this window with some pride.

"This," he had said, raising a jubilant arm toward heaven, "is our Mary window!"

There she stood in all her shining purity. And there she still stands—from whom God took flesh and whom he obeyed as a child. Clad in glory, there she waits, Sunday after Sunday, who under the inspiration of the Holy Spirit prophesied that all generations should call her blessed. Is there not a single voice of ancient custom to praise her? Is there no one in all that vast weekly throng to seek her intercession? No, not one. In this room only the attending angels on her window salute her: "Hail, Mary, full of grace!"

The rest is silence.

Convocation at Yale 22 April 1954

Speaking at the Yale Divinity School Convocation on *Changing Perspectives of Church History*, Roland Bainton sketched in a backdrop of oscillation. Down the ages, he said, the electricity of the spirit had flowed alternately in opposite directions: periods of corruption had been succeeded by stern reform, assimilation by withdrawal, simplicity by complexity, sectarianism by the desire for unity.

"What, then, is common to all periods?" he asked. "The personal realization of God, the continuity of the experiential."

Later, as we stood in line at the refectory, I said to him: "I cannot believe that our Lord was speaking only of the continuity of the experiential when he said that the powers of death would never conquer the Church. Without the continuity of the institutional and dogmatic, Christianity would have disappeared long ago."

The conversation shifted to the subject of the Oxford Movement. Dr. Bainton mentioned that late in life, many years after John Henry Newman "wrote himself over to Rome" with his *Essay on the Development of Christian Doctrine*, he met again with the head of the Anglo-Catholic movement, the pious Edward Pusey, and with its originator, the selfless John Keble. Their friendship had not dimmed, and they still held in common many deep, Christ-centered experiences.

As Dr. Bainton, my wife, and I sat at table together, he looked across at our blond two-and-a-half-year-old and remarked wistfully: "I shall never be able to teach her."

He has been teaching at Yale University for more than a generation. In eight years he will retire. A career of noted accomplishment has been his. He is considered by many to be one of the best historical lecturers and writers of American Protestantism. He has an impish habit of drawing caricatures of his friends while they eat, and so, when the conversation lagged, he took out his pad and pencil and set to work on a nearby dignitary.

Amos Wilder was also at the Convocation, and as he lectured

in the well-chiseled phrases of one who is both an artist and a scholar, his famous brother Thornton Wilder, the author of many classic novels and plays, looked up at him with furrowed brow from his humble seat in the congregation.

Such words as *kerygma* and *kairos, heilsgeschichte* and *weltanschauung* were floating cryptically through the air like so many flying saucers—strange, faint, glimmering discs of meaning, to many of us more mystifying than enlightening. Not that the lecturer was pedantic. On the contrary, he was simple, deep, and delightful. These foreign words are quite common in present theological discussion. But those who have lived long enough to outwear several such sacred vocabularies know full well how soon they will pass into the limbo of discarded coinage and called-in currency. Commenting upon this indurability, the lecturer recommended that in dogmatic position-taking "both sides practice candor and respect, speaking the truth, as they see it, in love." The danger, he said, is "unchristian and discourteous polemic."

Later, when the lecturer and the crowds had gone, I sought the familiar solitude of Marquand Chapel. Here in this lovely white sanctuary Marjorie and I had been married. We had met in our first weeks at the Divinity School and six months later had walked down the aisle of this chapel. Here we worshipped every morning with the other students. As I waited alone in the silence, there drifted to my ears on the winds of the past the militant male voices of the choir:

> He who would valiant be
> 'Gainst all disaster,
> Let him in constancy
> Follow the Master. . . .

And then the vibrant, spirited voices of the student congregation, sounding like a mighty army on the march, or again singing softly and harmoniously:

> O Jesus, I have promised
> To serve Thee to the end;

Be Thou forever near me,
My Master and my Friend. . . .

It was easy to believe in a Protestant form of the Christian faith in such an atmosphere. Here on this high hill everyone breathed an air of friendliness and forgiveness. Young hearts aglow in the first fresh devotion of lifelong commitment, young minds eagerly pursuing the dawn of truth—among such would-be saints, who could not believe in the "gathered" Church as a company of redeemed sinners? All together, in the unity of a single spirit, the students could forget the sharp divisions revealed in the last hour's theology class, as they sang forth their conviction:

We are not divided,
All one body we,
One in hope and doctrine,
One in charity. . . .

Drifting on the winds of the past, the echoes died away, and I was alone again, remembering . . . remembering how we had walked down the aisle a second time in this chaste white chapel. Here it was on a June day of 1951 that we were jointly ordained into the ministry of the Congregational Church. Our most beloved professors and friends in the ministry had laid their hands upon our heads, invoking the gifts of the Holy Spirit, and then Dr. Richard Niebuhr gave us the charge, our marching orders, which began:

BOTH
OUR DAINED

> It is not often that we are privileged by the church to ordain husband and wife to the Christian ministry. God, indeed, by the operation of his spirit, has set apart for this service many a couple and many a family. The church, however, follows God slowly and cautiously. Perhaps this is as it should be. Yet we may rejoice today that you have been called and ordained not separately but as one body, and that the charge may be addressed to you not separately and individually but as united in ministry to each other as well as in common ministry to others.

The third time we walked down the aisle of Marquand Chapel it was with a baby in our arms, coming for the rite of baptism. Dr.

Bainton, who had married us and taken part in our ordination, now touched our younger child with the waters of eternal life.

I remembered all these past blessings, and thanked God for each of them, and then I walked back up the aisle again, through the chapel doors and out into the present.

Science and Morality   23 April 1954

Magazines and newspapers this week carry lead articles on a great physicist and World War II leader in A-bomb production. He had Communist friends, and he opposed the development of the H-bomb. Question: is this another case of hidden disloyalty, or is this genius of an eremite merely one more fog-bound, muddle-minded liberal?

The pride of such a scientist has seemed all too often to be the pride of the man who would play God. Conditioned to habits of mind which look down from above in order to analyze and control the forces of nature, such scientists may well be the antithesis of the saints, who look up to surrender and be controlled by a power and an intelligence greater than their own. The habit of mind that spends most of its time looking down instead of looking up has gained increasing control of the post-medieval world.

For the last century men have been so busy mastering the outer nature of the world about them that their own inner natures have not been properly cultivated and developed. They have chosen to seek knowledge of this material world to the almost complete exclusion of self-knowledge and the wisdom of God. And now mankind is beginning to reap the whirlwind. For along with better living conditions and the blessings of physical health, experimental and industrial science have provided the implements of mass world suicide.

Whatever knowledge man possesses is always at the mercy of his character: it can be used for good or for evil. And science, if it is not to destroy all things, must be controlled by a higher moral force.

Where, then, is this higher moral force to be found? One of

the discouraging things about foremost Protestant theologians is the moral relativism and situation ethics with which they confuse their followers. General norms of behavior are only indicative, never universally binding, they say; for God speaks personally to each problem of conscience, at times even prescribing action contrary to the general norm. Thus is the Creator, who gave the natural law, accused of contradicting himself; while the wayfaring man, who looks for sure direction and solid ground under his feet, finds himself in the trackless wastes and swamplands of subjective preference, victimized by an arbitrary Tyrant who may in his case condone or command the inherently immoral.

That God does not customarily and by supernatural intervention solve the problems of conscience, confirming his divine decision by miracle, is self-evident. He meets men through his natural creation and the concrete circumstances of individual existence.

"The natural law and natural rights are nothing else than an expression of natural demands of God. An encounter with the natural reality of public life, of economics, of marriage and family life, is a personal encounter with God."[5]

Add to this the supernatural life and law revealed in Jesus Christ, and there are grounds enough for that sure moral guidance which the fantastic increase of modern scientific knowledge so desperately demands.

But Protestantism does not offer such specific and authoritative moral guidance. It says, "Maybe . . . perhaps . . . to the best of my knowledge . . . it seems to me . . . decide for yourself what is right and what is wrong in the matter of confession, abortion, sterilization, divorce, euthanasia, church-going, and the like, for God has here spoken no sure word of decision and direction."

Should we, then, be surprised when the man in the street concludes that all moral teaching is of merely relative validity and therefore unreliable?

Can we blame the fog-bound, muddle-minded liberal scientist for his ethical confusions, when we ourselves have nothing better to offer?

Defense by Derision   29 April 1954

Derision seems to be a chief defensive weapon in the arsenal of sectarianism. It provides an easy escape from the harder work of detailed examination and judicious thought.

"Well, Father, have you preached lately on the cardinal sin of gluttony?"

In calling one young friend's attention to the emotional prejudice of such anti-Catholic remarks, I provoked a barrage of low-church low-blows, which ended with the charge that anyone claiming to belong to "the one true Church" could not possibly possess the *sine qua non* of Christlike character, humility.

This came from a dedicated, likeable Protestant who never suspected how conditioned his responses were. Words such as "rosary," "mass," and "penance" produced reactions at the mouth as predictable as the salivation of Pavlov's dog. For these were plainly and patently "corruptions" and "accretions" introduced by "idolatrous Romanists."

I mentioned to this anti-Catholic friend that a certain elderly Congregational minister had visited us the same afternoon and had spoken in no uncertain terms of his ardent desire for the reunion of Christendom. In his earlier ministry he had united two Protestant churches in Vermont and had been active in the first days of the ecumenical movement. He saw denominationalism as a curse and a disease.

"The trouble with so many of our own ministers," he said, "is that they are infernally prejudiced on this question of local autonomy!"

"Freedom from dogma at any cost," I added, "even if it means complete loss of faith. Our congregations in many churches are starving for want of affirmation."

The elderly eyes twinkled with vitality. The chasm of half a century was annihilated in the meeting of our minds. We agreed that if the ecumenical movement was not going to dissolve in smoke, our low liberal churches, for their part, must repent and answer the call, "Come up higher!" We must accept bishops, for example, and definite credal teachings. We must even be so courageous as to re-examine our relationship to Greek Orthodoxy and Roman Catholicism.

"Yes, I suppose it is possible to affirm much more than we do without becoming narrow," he said thoughtfully.

We spoke of the coming Second Assembly of the World Council of Churches, which will meet this next August in Evanston, Illinois. He had little hope that any positive accomplishment in the way of reunion would emerge. He agreed with an editor of the *Christian Century* that

> the deliberative sessions of the ecumenical assemblies have studiedly ignored the sin for which in our prayers we professed repentance . . . the sin of our unhappy divisions . . . The World Council faces the grave danger of running into the sands of futility unless it attacks the ecumenical problem at its root.[6]

But what is this root problem? Is it perhaps the chronic sin of heresy and schism? For some time now a terrible suspicion has been lurking in my mind that we Protestants are such heretics and schismatics as were the ancient Arians, Donatists, and Cathari. They, too, defended themselves by derision. They too followed the example of Pilate's soldiers (Matt. 27:27–31) in mocking the Holy One of God.

My young anti-Catholic friend sees only arrogance and overweening pride in "the one true Church" position. But how much humility can there be in those who condemn this position without ever giving its spokesmen a fair hearing?

Off to Korea   10 May 1954

My serious, saintly friend W. McN. spent Saturday with us, and when Margaret's ear began to ache, he gave her his blessing —before we took her to the doctor's office for a shot of penicillin.

It has been raining steadily for nine days, and Saturday was no exception. W. McN. ate four plates of beans at the cherry drop-leaf table, while the rain pattered musically on the twenty-paned

window, and Margaret cried about her earache, and Mary Elizabeth accompanied her out of sisterly sympathy.

Once fed, we plied our black-suited guest with questions and
counter-arguments. He talked—somewhat haltingly, as might be
expected of a young and inexperienced priest—about the seven
sacraments as the ordained channels of grace, on the Immaculate
Conception and bodily assumption, on the reasonableness of the
mysteries of the faith.

Before he left, he promised to visit us again in seven years, that
is, at the end of his first hitch as a Maryknoll Missioner in Korea.
What a wonderful work he will do out there!

"It's too bad he had to be such a fine person," Marjorie commented after he had gone. "It would have been easier to dismiss
his ideas if he'd been the smooth, arrogant type."

Perhaps when he visits us again, I thought, we'll take it for
granted to call him "Father."

Bridging the Abyss   15 May 1954

Between Protestantism and Catholicism there is a black yawn-
ing abyss. One imagines it, at times, to be as wide as the infinite
qualitative difference that Kierkegaard posits between God and
man. If one is true, the other is *ipso facto* false.

Fighting against this fact, I become the impossible bridge. If
I am not to fall into the unfathomable emptiness below, I must
soon stand firmly on one side or the other. A destiny decision
must be made, and the Moment will not wait forever.

All Protestantism reduces itself in the end to Kierkegaard's dictum that truth is subjective.[7] Indeed, this is exactly where it also
began—in the horrendous tensions of Luther's scrupulosity. To
accept this view means in the end the loss of all revelation, order,
and sanity. Who, looking into the deceitfulness of his heart, can
hope to cast anchor in subjectivity? Unless there is an objective
order of truth beyond me, I am lost.

Yet Catholicism places the absolute point of contact here and
not beyond. Jesus Christ is God in the flesh, I verily believe, and

therefore cannot deceive us. But where shall I hear his sure and certain voice? In the Pope of Rome, a mere man like myself?

"Demonic *hybris*," cries Paul Tillich, who is said by many to be a reliable human bridge between Protestantism and Catholicism. Perhaps, if I read further into his works, he can show me how to assume such an awkward position with equanimity!

Roman thinkers recognize Tillich as the most impressive Protestant theologian in America. He once considered joining the Catholic Church, since he believes it is the better preserver of the substance of Christian revelation. But he could not stomach Rome's "absolutizing of the finite." He may well be the greatest heresiarch of our day.

Not being a spiritual genius myself, I stumble along as best I can, step by step, thankful for whatever light I receive. It is difficult for any of us to practice the humility of recognizing that our cherished preconceptions and guiding attitudes might, after all, be wrong. By the grace of God, I have at least come to the acknowledgement of my own ignorance and helplessness. Helpless because the end I seek is above my nature and can be arrived at only by supernatural means, as our Lord tells us in John three and six. The gift is all: there is an infinite disparity between this gift and our most heroic efforts. It is the difference between nature and the supernatural. Mere human striving must give way to utter reliance upon God Incarnate: for he alone can bridge this gaping ontological gulf.[8]

Sacrament of Penance   17 May 1954

"Confessional: A Protestant Possibility" is the title of an article by a Presbyterian minister in a recent issue of *In Context*, the Yale Divinity School's student publication. It calls for serious consideration of a Protestant confessional, saying that the chief obstacle to its establishment would be "the question of the minister's status."

It is evident that without an absolving priesthood no real confessional, conveying the pardon and peace of God, could ever be established. Such an empowered priesthood Protestantism does not have. It therefore offers substitutes, such as "pastoral counseling," which for its efficacy depends primarily, not upon the action of God but upon the personality and wisdom of the minister.

Jesus "knew what was in man" (John 2:25). He knew what had to come out of him before he could be at peace with God or his fellows. He therefore told his ministers: "Peace be with you." He who during his own earthly life forgave so many sinners then said this: " 'As the Father has sent me, even so I send you.' And when he had said this, he breathed on them, and said to them, 'Receive the Holy Spirit. If you forgive the sins of any, they are forgiven; if you retain the sins of any, they are retained' " (John 20:21–23).

This so plainly establishes sacramental confession that it is difficult to understand how any who pride themselves on following the Bible faithfully can ignore it. Certainly Martin Luther, more than any other man the founder of Protestantism, never sought to remove the confessional boxes from the Church. In *The Babylonian Captivity*, which attacked unsparingly the teachings of Catholicism, he wrote:

"Of private confession, which is now observed, I am heartily in favor . . . it is useful and necessary, nor would I have it abolished—nay, I rejoice that it exists in the Church of Christ, for it is a cure without an equal for distressed consciences."

Sin that is unconfessed and unforgiven poisons the unconscious, festers the faculties of the soul, creates a restless, anxiety-ridden approach to life. If we were all angels or saints, confession directly to God alone might satisfy us. But we are human, and we need to hear an authoritative voice declaring that our sins are assuredly forgiven, in the name of God and man.

Protestants, I am convinced, simply do not know what they are missing by continuing to reject the healing gifts and graces of the sacrament of Penance. They have gone so long on short rations that they think starvation is normal.

Entering the Ministry   19 May 1954

The summer of 1945 was a trying one. My father was sick, and I was uncertain about my vocation in life. I prayed about both problems. I read the New Testament continually, carrying individual books of it in my coat pocket. And someone steered me onto Kierkegaard: his rigorous message smote my conscience, stirred my heart and deepened my anguish. I was working as a reporter at the time, having recently returned somewhat shaken from my tour of duty as an American Field Service ambulance driver in Africa and Italy. I was troubled. I searched for meaning. Overseas I had seen men full of holes and full of evil. I had helped to put them back on their feet or down deep into the ground. I knew the frailty of life. I knew its fears. And I could not rest till I had found some stability beyond these things.

In September I called on Dean W., the kindly and efficient administrator of the Yale Divinity School. I told him that although I did not know what I wanted to do vocationally, it was my desire to enter the seminary and learn more about the Christian faith.

"What church do you belong to?" he asked.

"None," I replied. "I never got around to joining any."

His bushy eyebrows arched in surprise. "How did that happen?"

"Well, I went away to the Southern Arizona School for Boys at the age of twelve. Then at fifteen I transferred to Phillips Academy, Andover, for three years. So I was never around home long enough to attend a confirmation class in my parents' church. When I got to Yale College, neither the students nor the teachers I knew seemed to have any depth of interest in religion. So far as I saw, there was little concern about God and the state of one's soul. Occasionally I went to hear the visiting great preachers at Battel Chapel, but I guess what they had to say didn't sink very deep. Yet somehow a desire for light and truth did get planted firmly in my mind. In my junior year I wrote a semi-religious three-act tragedy called *Themistocles*. And that's about as close as I ever got to church membership."

Dean W. advised me to join the non-sectarian "Church of Christ in Yale University," otherwise known as Battel Chapel. Thus unaffiliated was I allowed to enter an interdenominational Protestant theological school with the understanding that I could decide upon a denomination later.

Andover and Yale are Congregational schools in origin and emphasis. So the most natural thing for me to do was to become a Congregationalist. Though I had vague Episcopalian leanings, I followed the line of least resistance into the fold I knew best of all. Many of the professors whom we held in high esteem belonged to this church and seemed to be satisfied with its latitude of belief and freedom from hierarchical interference.

In my years at the Yale Divinity School I came to know and love Jesus Christ more fully. I wanted to put my life, for what it might be worth, at his disposal. I considered the college chaplaincy but decided at last upon the parish ministry.

The Confession of faith that I read at my ordination examination followed the form of the Apostles' Creed. It contained this statement:

> The Holy Catholic Church is the society of those forgiven sinners everywhere who inwardly acknowledge Jesus Christ as their Lord and Savior. Where he is proclaimed and received in faith, there, and there alone, is the true church. This church is more than a company of believers: it is the Mystical Body of Christ. Its living bond of unity can be maintained only by God's Word and the witness of his Spirit, not by artificial restrictions imposed from without.

Like so many other seminarians of my day I really did not know what I believed about the Church. The doctrine did not even interest me. But it contained within its drab Protestant exterior a hidden time bomb.

Authority of Truth   20 May 1954

My Universalist friend, Rev. W. F., displays on his literature table a card titled *Avowal of Faith*, on which his church affirms its
belief, among others, "in the authority of truth, known or to be
known." I am in sympathy with this belief. I am not in sympathy
with Universalism.

My good "bishop and brother," Rev. J. E., Superintendent of
our churches, ends a recent piece in our denominational magazine
with these words: "We are bound together by chains of love and
mutual respect that we may 'walk in the ways of the Lord, known
or to be made known to us.' "[9]

W. F. and I play volleyball twice a week at the YMCA.
J. E. has often been a help to me, giving practical counsel from
his long experience in the field of churchmanship and from his
extensive knowledge of my own parishioners.

Both these Protestant ministers sincerely believe in the obligation of conscience to follow the authority of truth "known or to
be known." Of course, they themselves do not believe that there
is only one true Church . . . the Catholic Church.[10] But what of
those Protestants who come to believe that God has made such
a truth known to them?

The Preamble of our General Council's Constitution says this:
"We earnestly seek that the prayers of our Lord for the unity of
his followers may be speedily answered."[11] Joseph Sarto began
his pontificate as Pius X with just such a sentiment for his motto
—*Instaurare Omnia in Christo*. He, too, desired that all things
should once again be incorporated under the headship of Christ.
Indeed, what thoughtful follower of God Incarnate, surveying a
world in the torments of apostasy, does not utter such a prayer
early and late?

Suppose now he were to answer such prayers of my own by
leading me back to the great Mother Church and Fountainhead
of all Christendom. What would my Protestant friends have me
do if Roman claims ever came to bind my conscience? Only one

alternative would hew in honesty to the principles of Congregationalism: "reunion without tarrying for any."

Irresistible Attraction   24 May 1954

Is Roman Catholicism a totalitarian religion?

It gives its adherents ready-made beliefs on authority, so that
in the intellectual realm it does come between the believer's mind
and God, claiming to do so by God's will. But it comes between
them to join them, as a road runs between two towns, and not as
a wall of separation. In the realm of worship, however, a Catholic's prayer can go as directly to God as the Protestant's. In the
realm of politics the method of democracy presumes no specific
content of religious opinion. To put our Godward relationship
at the service of political purpose by asserting that every form of
Christianity must be democratically organized—this is in itself
a totalitarian attitude, a form of statist idolatry. It is, on the contrary, the rejection of heaven-sent authority that leads ultimately
to the human ant-heap and the dictator.

Does Roman Catholicism appeal only to the "authoritarian personality"? Strangely enough, most priests I have known habitually
urge their people toward self-reliance, telling them to stand on
their own two feet, trusting in God's ever-present help. Catholics,
it seems to me, are saved from subordination to social-climbing,
power-hungry laymen by the given-quantity of priestly control.
They are spared the tyranny of theological fashion, whether from
favorite professor or local preacher, because they have higher
models of sainthood and certitude of the truth. And it is lust for
truth, not desire for a dictator, which leads one to inquire into
the validity of Roman claims. As the recently-converted Chief
Rabbi of Rome, Eugenio Zolli, puts it: "The convert is one who
feels impelled by an irresistible force to leave a pre-established
order and seek his own proper way. It would be easier to continue along the road he was on."[12]

How much easier indeed! Having managed thus far a brazenly
independent existence, I would prefer to freewheel it down the

open highway forever. I work in a veritable garden spot and minor paradise. My parishioners, God bless them, are kind to me when I am kind to them, and they let me do my job as I see fit. This includes ample time for study, sermon-making and, most fun of all, playing with my children. We fill a genuine need here, making God real and interpreting his Word to a community composed predominantly of young couples with growing families. They work like beavers when it comes to church activities, such as strawberry suppers, candlelight services, pageants, bazaars, auctions, operettas, and parties. Their attendance at worship is not too bad, considering the apathy of New England in general. As in most small communities, some of them gossip too much about their neighbors, but on the whole, they are a well-meaning, friendly people. Why should I leave them for some will-o'-the-wisp?

And yet—this mysterious power of attraction burns within my bones and will not leave me. Is it, perhaps, the grace of God drawing me home?

Ascension Day   27 May 1954

Can our jet flight engineers ever break through the seemingly impenetrable thermonuclear barrier? Is the aviation industry getting anywhere fast? Answer: it is getting nowhere faster than anyone else. Hell-bent for a fog-bound horizon, its terminal port is "the wild blue yonder." It seems to have one major monomaniacal purpose: speed. Fleeing in circles around the circumference of a shrinking globe, it vainly chases its own tail-fins.

Socrates pursued death in a far different way. He was realistic. He sought fulfillment outside of this present world and thus was ever preparing to leave it. He was no shortsighted secularist, for he knew that the secret of this world's true good lay hidden in the next. He would have appreciated the advice of that desert demon destroyer, St. Anthony of Egypt: "Practice humility and contempt of the world, and remember that on the day of judgment you will have to account for all your deeds."[13]

Does the "good" American Catholic follow, even remotely, such foolish counsel (1 Cor. 1:25), or does he rather ape his decent pagan brother in the shrewd pursuit of secular shadows? What about the Roman clergy and hierarchy in this well-fed country? A Protestant minister said to me recently that the Catholic Church was a separate, self-righteous, and contradictory group within our society, a threat to our national unity. I waited in vain for him to conclude logically with some call to action, such as "Catholics to the lions!" But this never came—perhaps because he knew that most "good" Catholics are just as materialistic and earth-bound as their pagan and puritan neighbors—take to the skies in jet aircraft though they all may.

In some quarters there is a separatist American version of what it is to be a "good" Catholic, as standardized in its cheap mediocrity as our secular magazines and popular songs.

According to this banal ideal, the "good" Catholic not only fulfills his religious obligations like clockwork and leads an irreproachable life, but he also keeps to his own kind. He reads only Catholic books, all too often pious hackwork, and associates exclusively with those who have been stamped out of the same cookie cutter as himself. He knows little if anything about the long, rich tradition of Catholic culture. Narrow and uncreative, his timid conformity is far indeed from the spirit of the first apostles: "Now when they saw the boldness of Peter and John . . . they recognized that they had been with Jesus" (Acts 4:13).

Few of the homeless and wandering will ever be inspired to enter a city hidden in such a dark hollow. They search for a city on a high hill, a city whose bright battlements will gleam to them from afar. But all that their weak eyes are able to make out, when they look up, is an empty sky with no stars.

Roman friends, look to your saints for light! And "If then you have been raised with Christ, seek the things that are above, where Christ is, seated at the right hand of God" (Col. 3:1).

All Hope Abandon   3 June 1954

Hilaire Belloc, lucid and vigorous Catholic historian, tells us,

> For a whole lifetime after the movement called the "Reformation" had started (say from 1520 to 1600), men remained in an attitude of mind which considered the whole religious quarrel in Christendom as an ecumenical one. They thought of it as a debate in which all Christendom was engaged and on which some kind of ultimate decision would be taken for all.[14]

What hope is there now in our modern ecumenical movement among the non-Roman churches? In the foreign mission fields, where subtle sectarian differences were an obvious drawback, it had its beginning as an agonized cry for singleness of witness. The fact that the competing Protestant denominations held their contradictory beliefs "in all good conscience" was not a legitimate excuse to the heathen. Scripture told them that Christ had founded one Church: why, then, so many?

What hope is there for advancing the cause of Christian unity at Evanston? We are now informed that the problem will not even be considered this next August at the Second Assembly of the World Council of Churches.[15] It has been shelved in deference to the establishing of "good relations among the existing churches." But this is defeat confessed in advance! As one Protestant leader concludes, "In order to study and discuss church union, it is necessary to go outside of the World Council!"[16]

Where else can the defeated seeker of unity go but to Rome?

Scandalous Priest   4 June 1954

During my call on an ex-Catholic parishioner this evening, a story came out which I have heard more than once before. As a child of seven, my present parishioner had gone to confession without really understanding what it was all about. She had waited in line a-tremble with fear, listening to the priest yell angrily at some innocent playmate. When her turn had come, she had entered the dark box to recite her oft-repeated, standardized set of wrongdoings. "I hit my sister three times, I talked back to my mother four times, etc."

"What sins has a seven-year-old on her conscience?" Mrs. X. said to me earnestly. "Lots of the kiddoes used to make up lies to keep the priest happy. He scared us half to death. How could I respect such a man? Oh yes, he got the church out of debt by preaching about how empty the collection plate was every Sunday, but nobody liked him. He never came to call at our home, not even when my mother was dying—he sent one of his curates instead. They'd visit us once a year for the 'coal money,' and that was all. Here you come and talk with me as if I were a human being. The average Catholic can never really be friendly with his priest: they live on entirely different planes."

The image of the irate priest frightening a seven-year-old out of the Catholic Church—and that's what it comes to, though the response was a delayed one—this calls to mind our Lord's warnings: "Whoever causes one of these little ones who believe in me to sin . . ." (Matt. 18:6).

But the deeper question also rises: does the bad priest invalidate the institution *ipso facto*? Obviously not. Well then, is an authoritarian institution more apt to produce such wolves-in-sheep's-clothing than a freer church polity? Perhaps, since power does corrupt. Catholics are taught, however, that the priestly power resides in the office and not in the man. Still, the office is easily abused.

Desperately needed by pastors of all persuasions: the patience of Christ, who was humble and lowly of heart, and who laid his hands upon troublesome children in blessing.

Weeds Among the Wheat   5 June 1954

How many Protestants never seriously consider the claims of the Catholic Church through a feeling that she has lost the mark of holiness? There is a very real emotional difficulty here for those whose lives have been touched by the hypocrisy of bad Catholics. The Protestant imagination takes offense, and the Protestant mind refuses to work objectively.

Our Lord took his chances with the rest of humanity when he became a man. He risked the suffering of all our mortal frailties. He grew thirsty and hungry. He wept and was crowned with thorns.

He took his chances, too, when he founded a Church whose avowed purpose was to call and save the lost. He clearly foresaw what the result would be. Within that kingdom there would be both good and bad fish, wise and foolish virgins, tares and wheat —until the Last Day of separating judgment. Meanwhile, he said, "Lest in gathering the weeds you root up the wheat along with them. . . . Let both grow together until the harvest . . ." (Matt. 13:29–30).

The Church, then, is not an earthly heaven for the elect, nor a country club for the respectable and wealthy. It is a hospital for sick souls, in which sinners can become saints. As he said to the scribes and Pharisees who condemned him for associating with the dregs of society: "Those who are well have no need of a physician, but those who are sick; I came not to call the righteous, but sinners" (Mark 2:17).

Yes, Our Lord took his chances—even at the highest level. He knew there would be false shepherds, as well as false sheep. And yet among the first disciples only one of the twelve ultimately proved himself unworthy. Subsequent church history, I believe, shows an even higher percentage of loyalty than did that original nucleus of the chosen. On the average the standard of virtue maintained by popes, bishops, and priests has been remarkably good. Even so, there is no connection between high morality in the priest and the validity of the sacraments he distributes. If only holy men could convey God's gifts, the recipient would never know when he had actually received them. For every man's heart is hidden, and holiness of all things is most difficult to ascertain.

The chief aim of the Church is to produce this holiness. All Catholics are called to become saints. In the doctrines, command-

ments, counsels, and sacraments of their Church, they are provided with the necessary means of attaining that sanctity. Those
who neglect or flout these means of grace are usually the very
ones who cause the scandals of immorality which so offend non-
believers. The critic of Catholicism should ask himself: is it fair
to condemn any group for those of its members who do not live
up to the common code?

Catholics who give themselves to drink, lust, gossip, dishon-
esty, and corruption in politics—instead of to God—are a curse
on their Church. And yet Our Lord in his amazing mercy allows
them to remain in the fold, no matter how often they fall, if they
are genuinely penitent and sincerely desire to mend their ways.
Scandals and offenses though they be, they are not to be judged
by their brothers, to whom the Savior of all has said: "Judge not,
that you be not judged" (Matt. 7:1).

Personally, they would never frighten me away from the truth,
if truth is what the Roman Church offers. My chief difficulty as
to unholiness I find existing, not in others, but in myself. That
problem is one I can do more than talk about. That problem is
one I can fight to conquer, if I will. And it's quite big enough
to keep me busy for a long, long time to come.

Apostolate of the Laity   8 June 1954

From a Protestant retreat center in the Pocono Mountains of
eastern Pennsylvania comes the *Kirkridge Contour*, number 76 of
which begins:

> The word liturgy of course means "laywork" [Actually it means a
> *public* work: but there is a very great increase of lay participation
> in the Mass]; it is the part of Christian worship which the peo-
> ple are supposed to get under. Thus the Liturgical Movement in
> the Roman Church seeks more participation by the congregation.
> People, not just choirs, sing. Prayers are repeated in the vernacular,
> not in Latin, so that people can say them. Even the Communion is
> reinterpreted as the act of all who gather round the table, not just of
> the priest bringing the sacrament down by himself. Meanwhile this

very lay-participation which Roman Catholics encourage is slipping away in Protestantism.[17]

If the Roman gravitational pull ever landed me in their camp, it would be as a married layman. It is encouraging to think that God would still have a religious task for me of some sort. With the increase in lay participation there must be a growing number of faith-centered jobs the clergy cannot handle. Though I suppose if I had the courage of such convictions, I should then be willing to sweep the streets and scrub the piazza in order to be in the truth.

We were in a high place Sunday afternoon. My three young ladies and I—wife Marjorie, blond daughters Margaret and Mary—were driving leisurely toward Saint Joseph's Cathedral in Hartford, according to some whimsy of mine, and we saw that a service was going on inside. Marjorie had never visited the Archbishop's church, so we parked and entered. We stood uncomfortably in the back, saw that a large confirmation class was being examined, and started to leave. Marjorie noticed the balcony. Up we went. We soon found ourselves with the choir boys and two smiling nuns. What a magnificent view below! A thousand parents and friends, two hundred red-and-white-robed boys and girls. Margaret and Mary were all eyes! The candles glimmered from the altar. The stained-glass windows shone brightly. Ripples of laughter swept the great nave and echoed high in the arches, as a Monsignor poked fun at the children in his catechism check-up. Then at last they were marching out two by two, hands folded in attitude of prayer; while up in the balcony the high voices of the boys' choir followed precisely the delicate, rhythmical movement of a nun's hands.

A lovely and vivid memory! But down to earth again. . . A telephone call came this afternoon from a Mrs. L., saying that Father C. offered us two complimentary tickets to St. Catherine's Strawberry Supper tonight. (Our own Strawberry Supper last Thursday served three hundred.) So far I have had little contact with this new local priest, though I did call on his dying mother in the hospital a few months back, which he seems to have appreciated. His predecessor came to our 200th Anniversary in 1952 and said to the assembled throng of old-timers: "In these troubled days, when atheism, secularism, and communism assail us all, the churches have got to stand or fall together." Amazing sentiment from a priest! Far too liberal to please his superiors, I am afraid. But the Spirit bloweth where it listeth, and bishops cannot bind him! If he wishes more lay participation in the work of the Church, whether Catholic or Protestant, let us not frustrate his desire! It was Pius X who said, "What is most needed is to have in each parish a group of laymen who are virtuous, well instructed, and really apostolic."

Holy Spirit of God, guide us by your wisdom and lead us into your way, that all the faithful, each according to his measure, may become ministers of your grace and messengers of your love; through Jesus Christ our Lord. Amen.

One True Church   10 June 1954

Father C. had asked the three local Protestant clergymen and their wives to the Strawberry Supper at St. Catherine's Church. He led us on a guided tour of the sanctuary and rectory (after the sumptuous shortcake), explaining in detail everything from holy water to robe closet.

"This is the people's church: I just happen to be in charge," he kept saying.

His friendliness, candor, and democratic spirit were the opposite of the arrogant priest image painted by prejudiced anti-Catholics.

As we ate, my good friend, the local Episcopal minister, let slip some reference to "the one true Church," referring of course to all three allegedly Catholic branches.

"You mean *this*?" I asked with a quizzical smile, waving a hand to the four walls of the Roman basement in which we were eating.

"No, no, no," he answered in surprised exasperation. "Definitely not!"

The branch theory of the Protestant Episcopal Church has always struck me, even in my most unregenerate liberal days, as being way out on a dead limb. If the traditional Catholic position is correct, then the separated branches have no share in the visible body of the Church, failing as they do to accept the authority of the papacy in faith and morals, without which historic Catholic unity cannot be maintained.

That Episcopalians are Protestants and not Catholics is evident from their majority rejection of a sacrificing priesthood, the dogma of transubstantiation, the cult of Mary, the invocation of the saints, the seven sacraments, clerical celibacy, sacred images, indulgences, relics, purgatory, etc. From the traditional Catholic position Anglican orders have been declared invalid, and quite rightly so, since they represent and perpetuate a position which is patently Protestant.

Private judgment reigns supreme within the Episcopal fold, and this despite the salutary influence of the Apostles' and Nicene Creeds.[18] As one bewildered young Britisher saw it: "After the war, I'd go to one Church of England priest, then to another. One would say one thing, and another would say another. But they would all say: 'I think this, but that's just my opinion.' And that didn't seem right to me."[19]

The ungilded honesty of Quakerism, Congregationalism, and other non-high-collar societies is seen in their lack of precious pretense on such subjects as apostolic succession. Gathered churches admit that they are only voluntary associations of seeking freemen. They honestly recognize that they have no basis for claiming to be "the one true Church."

Martin Boegner, French leader on the Faith and Order Commission of the World Council, tells us that Holy Scripture "affirms one and only one Church of Christ, whose visible unity is part of the testimony she must render her Lord."[20]

Does such a single, unified, unifaithed *ecclesia* exist on earth today as Christ promised it always would, or has he been impotent to realize his expressed will and purpose?

Only the Roman Church possesses one authoritative faith and one external body. Is it, then, the continuing consummation of what our Lord originally instituted two thousand years ago?

Even those who say that the one true Church is yet to be realized (where has it been for lo these many centuries?) agree that the ecumenical movement cannot succeed without including Rome. But Rome is irreformable! Therefore, if this movement is to achieve Christian unity, the Protestant position, which is capable of change, must change—Romeward.

St. Thomas More   12 June 1954

What is the effect of a religious conversion on the friends of the convert? Sadness at the loss of a brother who now leaves the household; resentment at the trouble and confusion his changing of sides causes; apprehension lest his conscience be right and theirs be wrong. And if he bear witness too boldly, hatred. These emotions lie hidden behind that question which is ever asked of converts: "Why have you done this thing?"

"Having examined the claims of the Roman Church," comes the honest reply, "I am intellectually convinced of their truth. The deeper reason, of course, is the action of God's grace, enlightening the mind and strengthening the will."

"But I do not agree with you in this matter."

"That is your right and privilege. Every man must follow his own conscience. As for me, I can do no other, 'without the jeopardizing of my soul to perpetual damnation,'[21] as St. Thomas More put it."

What a gentleman in matters of conviction was that sixteenth-century Lord Chancellor! Henry VIII tried to force upon him an oath that required the acceptance of the king's religious supremacy and the repudiation of the authority of the pope. While refusing to desert the Catholic cause, More made no attempt to convert others to his position. He would not even give them the reason for his own dark decision.

> In my conscience this was one of the cases in which I was bounden
> that I should not obey my prince, since that whatsoever other folk
> thought of the matter (whose conscience and learning I would not
> condemn nor take upon me to judge) yet in my conscience the
> truth seemed on the other side.[22]

A prisoner in the Tower of London, he was subjected to intense but subtle pressure to declare himself openly for or against the king's usurpation of the pope's religious supremacy. Declare for it, his soul would be lost. Declare against it, his body would be destroyed. Like Christ before his tormentors, he kept his silence —though in his final trial, when he saw that his condemnation had been arranged in advance and was inescapable, he did state his position, appealing beyond the law of Parliament to "the general law of Christ's universal Catholic Church." On the scaffold "he begged them earnestly to pray for the king that he might have good counsel, protesting that he himself died the king's good servant, but God's first."[23]

Being most exceedingly distant from sainthood and its silences (though admiring such from afar off), I feel the necessity to set my innermost thoughts on paper. If the Catholic claims should ever bind my conscience with absolute certainty, these words will then serve as my own answer to the question: "Why have you done this thing?" Meanwhile, they help me clarify my thoughts. They give me something to fall back on when reason grows confused or memory dims. More apologetic than polemic, they are intended to be a mere personal record. I wish to reason into the truth, at this stage of writing, no one so much as myself.

Through God's providence, however, I believe that in time to come these words may aid other souls caught in the whirlpools of religious doubt by showing them more clearly that Rock which their fingers strive to grasp in a last desperate effort to save themselves from a watery grave of watered-down theology.

Catholicism or Chaos is what I call my objective carving of Roman doctrine, by which I seek to project my mind into a Catholic mode of thought in order to get a full and clear impression of what that really is. It seems to have been neglected lately in favor of these more personal *Threshold Thoughts*. Like a juggler, I have been trying to keep both balls in the air at once.

Then, too, there is the regular weekly study-and-sermon necessity, my primary creative obligation. What with pastoral calling, youth work, occasional weddings and funerals, church social activities, and far-too-infrequent periods of personal prayer —the doctrinal carving has for the moment been relegated to that uncomfortable pigeonhole labeled *Sins of Omission*. Thank God I believe in the forgiveness of sins!

Good and gentle St. Thomas More, if intercessions of the saints in heaven avail, pray for me that I may know God's truth and walk therein; through Jesus Christ, your Lord and mine. Amen.

Audience with the Pope   13 June 1954

On this day ten years ago in the morning, according to my Italian Journal, a Wac Lieutenant in a Rome perfume shop told me that the Pope was receiving soldiers at open audience from 11:30 A.M. to 1 P.M. I hitched a ride to St. Peter's Square in a French jeep, walked up long steps past natty Swiss guards, and with a hundred other gum-chewing, gun-toting Yankees entered into a large papal audience chamber.

When they carried Eugenio Pacelli into the crowded hall, he was sitting in a long white robe on a red-cushioned chair. The soldiers clapped. He bowed amiably, spoke briefly, and then both in Latin and English he gave us his blessing. I saw that the soldiers in front were kneeling as they kissed his ring.

A priest at the doorway was handing out rosaries previously blessed by the Pope. They came in small white envelopes on the front of which the papal seal was imprinted in gold. I asked him for three: two I gave to Catholic friends, the third is filed away with my Italian souvenirs.

The audience was over. The soldiers chatted and jostled each other as they filed through the doorway. Clutching my rosaries,

I went out again into the glorious Italian sunlight. I had seen the Pope.

Communism or Christianity   14 June 1954

An elder statesman of Quakerism writes in this week's *Christian Century*: "A weak, divided, uncertain Christianity can do little in the face of a strong, united, certain communism."[24]

The certain demonic zeal of those who hate God can be conquered only by the certain divine zeal of those who love him truly. The false doctrines of Karl Marx can be conquered by the reality-teachings of Jesus Christ, but only when these true teachings are brought into life earnestly, selflessly, heroically, by men and women who are all out for God, cost what it may.

Ordinary milk-and-toast Christianity just won't do in this extraordinary time of troubles. The foundations are shaking under our feet. The very skies overhead may tomorrow morning, or this evening, be filled with enemy wings. We can no longer afford to give lip service to Christianity while our hearts follow the ways of a pagan world.

Such a worldly spirit within the household of faith gave rise to Communism in the first place. It is a product of our own Western civilization. Its philosophy is German, from Hegel the rational idealist and Feuerbach the atheistic materialist. Its economics are English, based on a first-hand study of British labor conditions published by Engels in 1845 under the title *Conditions of the Working-Class in England*. Its sociology is French, for it was Proudhon who told Karl Marx that he was way up in the air with his abstractions.

This is Communism—the product of western Europe, as indeed are we also. It shares with us our God-ignoring materialistic bias. Yet it goes us one better by claiming that not only are matter and economics primary, but that spirit, and the other world of God which we call heaven, far from being of paramount importance to men, do not even exist.

Communism is the most dangerous Christian heresy our civilization has seen since the invading hordes of Islam were turned back after partial conquest of the European continent. Its doctrines are a twisting, a perversion, and a contradiction of the truth as revealed by Jesus Christ.

Communism tells us that there are three basic realities in life: raw materials, tools, and labor. The relationship among these three makes the course of history, which is a mighty self-determining force whose purpose it is to raise the proletariat to the seats of power and eventually to bring in the utopian classless society. (Note the surreptitious inclusion of *purpose*, a spiritual force, in a supposedly all-material system.)

Christianity tells us that the basic reality is a Triune God. He created the material realm about us and the immortal souls within us by the *fiat* of his word and out of nothing. God wishes to save us from the subsequent corruption of this world, so that we might enter into heaven and serve him there forever.

Communism says that man has no destiny beyond this earth and no final Judge. Thus morality, conscience, the sense of right and wrong—all this is merely relative to the class struggle. Lenin admits: "We do not believe in external principles of morality. Truth is what will advance the party and the revolution."

Right and wrong is determined by the Kremlin in Moscow, which teaches infallibly that anything goes. This includes murder, treachery, and terror, if they will help the purpose of world revolution.

Christianity teaches that all its moral standards, from the Ten Commandments on down through the new revelations of Jesus Christ, are derived from absolute and objective values located in the mind of God. No morality can be effective or enduring apart from faith in God who is the source and sanction of right and wrong.

These are the kind of diametrically opposed positions taken up by Communism and Christianity. The former spreads its pack of lies with a passionate dynamism of missionary conviction. The latter, for the most part, hobbles along halfheartedly. Because the fires of our faith have gone out, this new heresy attracts many by its burning sense of purpose and its heroic challenge to sacrifice.

Those with eyes to see and minds to think are well aware that "a weak, divided, uncertain Christianity can do little in the face of a strong, united, certain communism." But where is godly strength to be found for our worldly weakness? Where must we look for that cohesive unity which alone can conquer our festering divisions? Who, in exchange for our dark doubts, will offer us the unwavering light of certain truth?

General Council   24 June 1954

Twenty-five hundred Congregational Church delegates from all over the country are meeting this week at Yale University in New Haven. As an usher, it has been my job to see that only blue card bearers enter Woolsey Hall downstairs, and to pass out reams of printed literature, mimeographed amendments, etc. As a voting delegate, I must choose between those church union enthusiasts who favor a merger of our denomination with another and those anarchists obsessed with local autonomy who oppose the merger.

Between sessions I sit in a corner of the book display room to read-without-buying a copy of an ex-priest's declaration of independence and exposé of the Catholic hierarchy, hoping against hope that I will find some cure for "Roman fever."

The author was a Franciscan who became the head of a hospital in Phoenix, Arizona, and in that capacity did a remarkable job of human service. His superiors, however, feared that he was becoming a worldly priest, careless of his spiritual duties and mission, overemphasizing the material betterment of the needy and the physical healing of the sick. His Provincial Council decided that he should return to church work, lest he spoil on the job:

> In our judgment and by our decision, you may no longer serve in the capacity of superintendent of St. Monica's hospital, as we are convinced that it has led to the spiritual neglect of your Negro

parishioners and to laxities in your manner as a Franciscan and a priest.[25]

He refused to accept this decision. He called his priest friends together and told them he was resigning. Some wept, some blessed him, others openly cursed and damned him. Many vain entreaties and threats followed. His brother wrote him: "Doesn't the anomaly strike you?—alleging your loyalty to Christ as a justification for violating your solemn vow of obedience? Doesn't it strike you that *that* in itself, is a rejection of Christ?"[26] He mails his letter of resignation November 29, 1948. He marries one of his hospital workers August 13, 1949. He writes this book decrying the moral abuses and transgressions prevalent within his former fold. His exposures seem genuine enough. Such examples of priestly uncharitableness, greed, false accusation, unreasonable cruelty, sexual laxity, fear-enforcing tyranny, and power lust, if true, are most discreditable to the Roman Church. But it does not therefore follow that "the doctrine of Roman Catholicism could not be true if the hierarchy were false,"[27] that is, given to weaknesses of the flesh and spirit like the rest of mankind. Did not Christ himself predict that there would be tares among the wheat, bad fish in the net along with the good? Are not these very immoralities proof, perhaps, of the Catholic Church's divine secret and source? For without God's upholding and undergirding power, such a hierarchical institution, if it were merely human, would have died out long ago.

In the assembly hall the delegates to the General Council of Congregational Christian Churches heard at their opening meeting several scathing and supercilious references to the absurdities of Catholic superstition. Rome had enunciated and promulgated a new method of making holy water, said the speaker: the priest should draw the usual dirty liquid from his faucet and then boil all hell out of it!

This afternoon I sat beside C.C., an old undergraduate classmate of mine. He reminded me once again how I had first happened upon the intricacies of theological verbiage. As a $25-a-

week reporter on the *New Haven Evening Register*, I had been
sent up to the Yale Divinity School to cover the Lyman Beecher
Lectures of 1945. My undergraduate classmate, then a theological student, was present at these lectures, and he claims that I
approached him with a typical pagan question: "Who is this guy
Rheingold Kneebower anyway?"

I have since learned to have the greatest respect for Reinhold
Niebuhr, having studied under him at Union Theological Seminary one summer. Even in 1945 I must have known who he
was. As an undergraduate at Yale in those halcyon days before
Pearl Harbor, I heard him often. I can remember enjoying the
wide sweep of his cosmic gestures and the piercing look of his
eyes as he preached in Battel Chapel. But war can erase many
lesser memories. So perhaps I had for the moment forgotten the
image that eminent name should have recalled.

In All Directions   25 June 1954

A "fraternal delegate" from a Universalist Church greeted the
General Council yesterday with the assuring news that his own
brand of indefinite nothingness would "supersede conventional
Christianity." Taking the all-religions-are-equally-true tack, he delivered the delectable dictum that there would eventually be "no
barriers of creed, saviors, Bibles, or techniques of religious practice."[28] Thus did he seek to throw out the windows of Woolsey
Hall both the New Testament and the Savior of the world.

Congregational churchmen may be authority-shy, but why under God's heaven must they invite into their midst such non-
Christian spokesmen of anarchy unlimited? The talk goes on and
on about the nine possible forms of Church union,[29] while at the
same time such anti-Church propagandists are welcomed, wined
and dined. This General Council gets to be more and more like
that distraught horseman who bounded into his saddle and "gal-
loped off in all directions."

One booklet distributed to the delegates carries this comment
on the ecumenical question:

To many persons organic union appears as the ultimate goal, and the only satisfactory solution, of church unity. It may begin with two or more denominations, but the purpose frequently expressed is the eventual inclusion of all Christian bodies. The implications of such a purpose are far-reaching. Complete organic union of the Christian Church would obviously require union with the Roman Catholics.[30]

A little further on it says:

Few, if any, are ready to suggest that the free churches should unite with the Roman Catholic Church. No discussion of union can be complete, however, without thinking realistically about the place of this largest branch of the church in the ultimate scheme of things.[31]

Bravo! Let us so do.

Swan Song   1 July 1954

The Minister of the General Council delivered an address *Christ on his Throne* in which he stated the classical Congregational position, claiming that our churches "have and use a common interpretation of what Christ demands of them and desires his Church to be." I cannot agree with this statement: Congregationalists are not like-minded; they are anti-dogmatic liberals.[32] The rejection of doctrinal and ecclesiastical authority is central to their position. What this means in practice, I now see, is the reduction of belief to the lowest common denominator, indifference to objective truth, consequent vagueness and blind uncertainty, with the gradual surrendering of one apostolic teaching after another.
Writes one clear-sighted analyst:

There are those who denounce "dogma," and say that they can only believe in an undogmatic religion. They are apparently unconscious that they are talking nonsense. "Dogma" means formulated belief. It is just as much "dogma" to say "I believe in a God," or indeed to say, "I do not believe in a God," as it is to say, "I believe in the propositions of the Nicene Creed." To say, "I believe in religion without dogma" is to say "I believe, but I don't believe in anything in particular."[33]

Most Congregationalists think it doesn't matter what a man believes so long as he leads a good life. They agree to differ "where others feel bound in conscience to insist on some definite convictions to the exclusion of destructive denials."[34] "As long as you live a Christian life," they say, "it doesn't matter what you believe. Your actions are what count, not what you think in your mind."

But beliefs determine actions; ideas have consequences. The health of a tree's root determines the health of its fruit. "Every way of a man is right in his own eyes, but the Lord weighs the heart" (Prov. 21:2). God rewards the man who follows truth. His whole universe reacts against the man who follows falsehood. It is true, for example, that the law of gravity will pull a man down to the earth and kill him if he jumps off the top of a church tower. Some madman might conceivably climb up there and say in effect: "We all have a right to our own opinions. My ideas are just as right to me as yours are to you. And frankly, I don't believe in your so-called 'law of gravity.'" So off he jumps, and God soon lets him know who's right and who's wrong.

It is exactly the same in the realm of moral law. A man says to himself: "Who does this Moses think he is, telling me 'Thou shalt not commit adultery'? And who does this Jesus think he is, telling me 'If you lust after a woman in your heart, you are already guilty of adultery'? I don't believe in that old-fashioned nonsense. I'm a free man," says such a moral relativist. "I live in a free country, and I believe in free love." So off he goes merrily on his own way, until his wife and his children lose faith in him, his home breaks up on the rocks of infidelity, and he is left to spend his last days in lonely bitterness of soul.

In the doctrinal realm consequences of wrong belief become evident more slowly. But they are just as certain and twice as disastrous in their far-reaching effect. The political totalitarianisms of today are a direct consequence of the Reformation breakup of medieval unity, though almost half a millennium has intervened. The hammer wielded in 1517 at Wittenburg has now at Moscow joined itself to the sickle.

"Beloved, do not believe every spirit, but test the spirits to see whether they are of God; for many false prophets have gone out of the world." (1 John 4:1). Christ said to his chosen apostles: "Go therefore and make disciples of all nations . . . teaching them to observe all that I have commanded you . . . He that believes and is baptized will be saved; but he who does not believe will be condemned" (Matt. 28:19–20; Mark 16:16). St. Paul warned a duly authorized successor of those first apostles: "If any one teaches otherwise and does not agree with the sound words of our Lord Jesus Christ and the teaching which accords with godliness, he is puffed up with conceit, he knows nothing . . . imagining that godliness is a means of gain" (1 Tim. 6:3–5).

Such, I am coming increasingly to feel, is Congregationalism, which instead of teaching all things, abandons all things. The General Council, in its swan song finale yesterday morning, could not even pass a resolution in defense of the traditional Trinitarian teaching. Dr. Visser 't Hooft, Secretary General of the World Council of Churches, had spoken magnificently on the Evanston theme, *Christ Our Hope*. In an attempt to put the General Council on record as favoring the entry of Unitarians and Universalists into the World Council, a resolution was presented in disapproval of the "basis" formula of the World Council, *Jesus Christ Our God and Savior*. A proposed substitute resolution in favor of "the prevailing theological basis of the World Council," which is in effect Trinitarian, was presented by a group of neo-orthodoxish young-bloods. Neither motion passed; both were "referred to the Executive Committee for further study," a euphemism for "failing to witness to the faith."

Such is Congregationalism, as I now see it. Its adherents are, for the most part, sincere, likeable, intelligent, earnest, responsible, kind-hearted, well-intentioned—and disastrously mistaken.

Maryknoll Option   2 July 1954

A letter from the young missionary priest suggests that I drive over to Maryknoll, New York, to see one of his professors about my theological difficulties. As I, too, have the greatest respect for my Divinity School professors, I can understand this desire, but I hesitate to get involved in such a definite way. I met W. McN. one day in New Haven when I was looking over St. Thomas More Chapel—a chance encounter. To make a long trip to Maryknoll when I am full of uncertainties and doubts would seem to be jumping the gun. Perhaps I'll do that after I finish this book. If I were not working as a Protestant minister, I suppose I could take a trial course of instruction with some priest. But as it is, I shall simply have to work things out for myself through study and prayer. The Mary question troubles me, and I should put a great deal of concentration in on this and other difficulties before consulting anyone. Then, too, perhaps there is some small degree of hope to be found at Evanston. At any rate, I think it best to let the Maryknoll option await the outcome of the World Council of Churches meeting and this book. Marjorie is especially eager that I go to Evanston. After urging me to write to Father J. McC. immediately, W. McN. ends his letter: "I am finishing my retreat today. Will leave for San Francisco on July 3 and sail for Korea July 7. Remember us in your prayers. I am praying for your special intention."

Our Lord's Intention   6 July 1954

At General Council last week in New Haven I asked a professor who had been close to us at Yale Divinity School if he thought that Christ had meant the Church to be one. He answered: "Yes, if he intended to found a Church, he probably meant it to be one. But I am not at all sure that he ever intended to found a Church."

Dr. Niebuhr is both a "brain" and a saint. I would not presume to question his deep-thoughted sincerity. But very few New Testament experts, we are told, would now deny that Jesus both intended to found a Church and set about building it. Such a denial makes utter nonsense of the whole gospel record and is irreconcilable with the dogma of Our Lord's deity. Why else did he enlist disciples and carefully instruct their chosen inner circle? After his departure, the apostles continued his work because I think they *knew* that their Risen Leader purposed through them to build his Church. Under the guidance of his Holy Spirit they were soon busy perpetuating it. And that's good enough for me.

Dr. Visser 't Hooft, Secretary General of the World Council of Churches, says this: "As we read the New Testament we discover not many churches but only one church, one people, acknowledging one Lord."[35]

St. Thérèse of Lisieux   10 July 1954

People whose jobs involve too much thinking should scrub floors in their spare time. Dish-washing, diaper-changing, gardening, painting and the like are all valuable antidotes for busy-brains.

Indeed, balanced thinking demands balanced living. It cost Our Lord a good many years of quiet carpentry to come up with his priceless parables. And there is no evidence on record that he was ever a bookworm. I fancy that one of the chief things he loved about St. Thérèse of Lisieux was that she fed daily upon the gospels and felt no call to the drudgery of groping through scholarly tomes. In her *Autobiography* she wrote:

> Leaving to great and lofty minds the beautiful books which I cannot understand, still less put into practice, I rejoice in my littleness because . . . I see it is enough to acknowledge one's nothingness and surrender oneself like a child into God's arms . . . I close the learned treatise which tires my brain and dries up my heart and I turn to the Sacred Scriptures.[36]

How often I have longed to do just that while studying the claims of the Catholic Church! Especially when I have found myself delving beyond my depth. Not that I would underrate the uses of intellect or the age-moving achievements of mental giants like St. Thomas Aquinas. We thank God for the many great thinkers and writers he has sent. But fortunately he does not cut us all from the same pattern and cloth. He gives us our separate, individual callings within the unity of his Church, insisting, however, that whatever our calling, we fulfill it—like St. Thérèse—with the humility of a little child.

Fleeing Truth 31 July 1954

Home on vacation in Pennsylvania, on this morning of my thirty-third birthday, my father's nervous tread woke me up far too early. One of the children was soon crying, and the cocker spaniels barked anxiously.

I remembered how last night, sitting out in the sweltering back-yard heat, my mother had said: "Why should a seventy-two-year-old woman suddenly want to turn Catholic?" I had merely asked her what experiences she had had with Roman Catholics: had any of them ever talked to her about their beliefs? "No," she had answered. "Most people don't care about such things." She herself is an active Protestant churchwoman.

"What could I do if I weren't a minister?" I asked my father. "Why would you ever want to leave the ministry?" he replied. "You're happy where you are, and you'd better stay there." My father is almost seventy-eight, the same age as the Pope. Some of the time he is not well, but he still pursues his work with persistence and enthusiasm.

I believe my parents will accept whatever decision is eventually made. They have always lived for their four children and dozen grandchildren, and they still do. But at this point they might be quite surprised and troubled if they were to learn of my serious and prolonged inquiry into the whys-and-wherefores of Romanism.

Personally, I am still of two minds, driven by disturbing doubts and the buried memory of intransigent attitudes. In love with the saints—Ambrose and Augustine, Benedict and Bernard, Catherine and Clare, the two Theresas, and all the myriad golden names of the carefully canonized—attracted by such heroes and heroines of holiness, I dislike myself for what I am, a sinner in the line of Adam, a noxious compound of misery and nothingness, an immortal animal with high spiritual persuasions and egocentric character traits. By dint of past sickness and suffering, and by the grace of God, I have been forced to pursue fleeing truth—yes, even through purgatorial fires—with some persistence and a little prayer. Yet fearing perversely that I may catch my quarry, I now plot how to continue a while longer in my comfortable, impenitent, Connecticut compromise, if and when firm Catholic conviction ever comes. Could I not justifiably pass another profitable Protestant year trying to write a book on the lives of saints? What shall I do for a living and a way of life? This dreadful occupational uncertainty blocks my path like a great mountain.

So it is that I would sleep on and on and on. Too early my Father walks by, and dreamlike, far away I hear his voice, and I wonder what he wants of me.

Asleep in Siena   2 August 1954

Last night ten years ago, according to my Italian Journal, the New Zealand troops of the British Eighth Army, better known as "Kiwis," put in a ferocious attack for the last hill overlooking Florence. They were thrown back two hundred yards from the top. This I learned at San Casciano in Val de Pesa, where I climbed up into an observation post atop the Fascist City Hall and through my field glasses caught sight of pink Florentine towers in the sun and the smokepuff explosion of our shells on the surrounding hills.

The previous day I had driven from Castiglione di Lago through Orvieto on its rugged sentinel rock to the walls of Siena. Just outside the city gate I had parked my American Field Service ambulance, which served also as my bedroom. The next morning I woke early and walked at a leisurely pace through the medieval serenity of that lovely Tuscan town. At that time I knew next to nothing about St. Catherine of Siena. But of late I have been reading Sigrid Undset's masterful biography. If I had only cared more about the saints and less about the sights ten years ago in Italy, I might have held such sentiments as those of Blessed Raimondo of Capua, Catherine's confessor, when he said:

> Oh Lord, your mercy is boundless! How good you are towards those who understand you! But what must you be for those whose thirst you quench so miraculously! Lord, I do not think that those who have no experience of such wonders can understand them—I know that I cannot. We only know them as the blind know colors, and the deaf, melodies. But in our attempts not to be entirely ungrateful we ponder over and admire the great gifts of grace which you give so generously to your saints, and to the best of our ability offer our poor thanks to your majesty.[37]

On Pilgrimage 4 August 1954

An Episcopal bishop has just proclaimed that a return to the Catholic Church is the only means of merging the many sects now seeking unity through the World Council of Churches.[38] How sweet for him that he already belongs to this true Church, *he believes!* What a shock if he should ever conclude himself to be as much cut off from the Mystical Body of Christ as the uncouthest of country Congregationalists!

Writes a Roman Catholic: "The Protestant churches are unwilling to recognize the only source of unity possible, namely, a supreme authority representing Christ."[39] In other words, the ancient and authentic Catholic position is this: no pope, no unity.

How far the Evanston gathering will diverge from this position, I do not know. But I shall attend it as a private prayerful observer, doing my best to be open-minded, searching for a ray of hope.

Of Time and Eternity 7 August 1954

In central Italy there is a small mountaintop village named Capracotta, which overlooks the valley of the Sangro River. In December 1943 there was fighting down below in the valley. The snow was heavy, and they had to bring the wounded up the steep winding trail by mule-back. It was a rough four-hour journey, and many died of exposure on the way up to the Regimental Aid Post.

Most of the homes in the valley below Capracotta were rubble, and every day the eighty-eight shells, sounding like freight trains as they rumbled overhead, made new heaps of stone. One cold night shortly before Christmas the soldiers in that mountaintop outpost were ordered to stand-to. A German attack was expected at any hour. In order to warn the English commander of the new troop movements and the heavy guns Jerry was bringing up on the far side of the mountain, an old Italian peasant and his ailing wife had waded the icy river and slipped across the no-man's-land of that valley below.

Inside the Regimental Aid Post a young British doctor sat gazing at the fire. He was thinking of his wife and child back in England. He seemed suddenly to have a premonition and a dread, for he looked up, smiling uneasily, and said in his British way: "It's a bad do. It's a bad do to be dying in a strange land far from home."

We are *all* fighting and dying in a strange land far from home. As we sit by the fire thinking of the old familiar faces, the friends who have walked into the room of our life and gone out again, the lost dreams of our youth, and all the persons and places that have fled into the recesses of the past—as we remember these fleeting images, we, too, have a premonition and a dread: for we know that Death has marked us each for himself. We know that all things on the surface of our planet are forever changing and dissolving and forming anew. We know that the might and knowledge and fashions and riches of this world are insecure. We do not want to die and remain forever in the cold ground of a strange land far from home, for we know that across the dark ocean of death and beyond the last horizon there is a better country and a happier life.

And yet we mortals cling to time, fearing the unknown. "Millions of pounds for an inch of time!" cried Elizabeth the First, Queen of England, on her death bed—broken old Elizabeth, who had squandered half a century in political connivings and worldly intrigue.

The great men of the past, men of artistic genius, men of purse and power, men of humanitarian accomplishment—no matter what the strength of their life, they all succumbed to a very little noise, the tick of the clock. None of them could conquer time —except One. One by one the strong princes of this world have fallen. The shadow of the Adolf Hitler who strutted so ferociously down the Wilhelmstrasse has now faded into the history books. And Mussolini, whose thirst for glory led him to unleash the furies of modern warfare against the helpless tribesmen of Abyssinia, who was forever giving pompous speeches from a high Roman balcony, thrusting out a meaty chin and a stiff arm at the howling crowds below—where is he now? His body, which hung by its feet in the Piazza Loretto in Milan, lies in a nameless grave.

Where are all the brief Caesars of the past? Have they, too, not withered with the grass and faded with the flower?

When the great Italian painter Raphael died at the age of thirty-seven, they carried his magnificent painting "The Transfiguration," never completely finished, in the funeral procession, as a symbol of the incompleteness of life and the brevity of time.

The sun rises, and the sun goes down. The years slip away one after another: like snow at the end of winter, they disappear and are gone. The rivers run ceaselessly to the sea, and the remembrance of former things is soon forgotten.

We are strangers and pilgrims on the earth: our home is beyond. And yet we mortals cling to time, fearing the unknown. The game is a losing one—until we give it up and welcome Eternity with open arms—here and now.

You Shall Be as Gods   8 August 1954

One of the most dangerous illusions of our time has been the belief that man, by concentrating all his attention and energies on this world, to the almost complete disregard of supernatural realities and his own eternal destiny, would be able to perfect this world and make it a paradise on earth. This illusion of inevitable progress by virtue of man's self-sufficiency has infected the thinking of liberal philosophers for the past two centuries. It springs from man's rebellious pride, from his refusal to acknowledge the Lordship of God over his own life. Modern man would play the part of the Almighty: he himself would be the savior of his own being and the world about him.

The height of this modern pretension was reached in the philosophy of Karl Marx and his followers. They assure us that all progress comes from the proletariat, which is destined to save human society. It was not by chance that the Soviet Congress at the time of Lenin's death issued a statement containing this tribute: "Nikolai Lenin was the greatest leader of all times, and of all peoples. He was the Lord of the new humanity, the savior of the world." This was written in the spirit of the antichrist, which would shake the very powers of heaven, exalting itself even above the throne of God.

The whole of the modern world is infected with this attitude, not least of all we Americans. A friendly and generous people, energized greatly by the spirit of Christian charity, we are nevertheless proud, immature, and self-lauding. Asiatics and Africans looking at America often choose to see only our worse side. They see us as a nation driven by envy and greed for the gross material things of life. They note that we are a restless people, always on the go, burning up the highways in search of some faraway pleasure. And as we ride those highways, our selfish desires are continually inflated by an endless parade of hideous billboard advertisements, whose chief purpose is to make us want "what we don't need and can't afford." Is it any wonder that homes are disrupted by squabbles over money, that easy divorce and juvenile delinquency are on the increase? In this God-fearing country of ours much more money is being spent every year on alcoholic beverages than is spent on all our religious and welfare institutions put together. And our super-sunny optimists still believe in the inevitable progress and social betterment of the American way of life!

If God is going to save our nation from moral decay, he must first undermine and sweep away the false foundation of human self-sufficiency. This is why we live in a time of shaking foundations, as Paul Tillich has said, when the very ground under our feet seems to tremble. God is shaking the world that only those things which are firmly founded and of lasting value may remain (Heb. 12:27). God is saying to us what he said through the prophet Jeremiah to another rebellious, man-centered epoch of history: "Cursed is the man who trusts in man and makes flesh his arm, whose heart turns away from the Lord. The heart is deceitful above all things, and desperately corrupt; who can understand it? I the Lord search the mind and try the heart, to give to every man according to his ways, according to the fruit of his doings. Blessed is the man who trusts in the Lord, whose trust is the Lord" (Jer. 17:5, 9, 10, 7).

Evanston and Mary   15 August 1954

The Evanston Assembly of the World Council of Churches is truly an extraordinary gathering. The fifteen hundred delegates registering yesterday at Northwestern University's Patten Gymnasium came from six continents and forty-eight countries. The crossfire of unfamiliar tongues made it seem for a moment like a re-creation of the tower of Babel, though the delegates might prefer to remember Pentecost. Some of the strange ecclesiastics wore ornate breast crosses surmounted by wavy black beards. There were many colorful vestments and an even greater variety of conflicting theologies.

I asked an Englishman about his violet bib. "My name's Newbigin. I'm from India," he said. "Our bishops all wear this color of stock."

I spoke to a tall brown man in a long pinkish garment roped about the middle. He said his name was Chrysostom. "Are you also a golden-mouthed preacher?" I asked him. "My name, young man, has a denotative, not a connotative, value," he replied.

These two Indian representatives came from a land where the caste system still prevails. They went through the same registration line as the delegates from South Africa, where racial discrimination is the established practice.

Churchmen from behind the Iron Curtain, where atheism is the state teaching, remained as silent as possible, lest they be misrepresented or stumble into words which would cost them dearly on their return to their Communist homelands. Bishop Otto Dibelius, according to this morning's press, brushed aside questions about his East Berlin churches, while Pastor Guenter Jacob was careful to make it clear that he has had "complete religious liberty in the eastern zone and that the Communists permit him to preach whatever and whenever he wishes."[40]

This afternoon the opening plenary session will be held at McGraw Hall. This evening over 100,000 are expected to gather at Soldiers' Field for the spectacular Festival of Faith. This will be a significant and memorable day in the history of Protestantism.

It has, however, another dimension which most of the delegates will pass over lightly. Perhaps the Anglo-Catholic and Greek Orthodox among us will remember it. This day is not only the opening day of the Second Assembly of the World Council of Churches; it is also the day of the Feast of the Assumption of the Blessed Virgin. It is a *double entendre*, and as such, it may have been designed by Almighty God to point out with crystal clarity the cosmic abyss dividing Catholics and Protestants.

If Mary, who gave the Second Person of the Blessed Trinity that human flesh with which he would redeem this fallen world, was throughout her life preserved by God's special grace from the taint of sin, in order that his mother might be worthy of him; and if, being untouched by darkness, her pure body was taken up into the light of eternity after her death—then, by failing to include her in their prayers and by disdaining to call her blessed, Protestants omit from their lives a prime source of intercessory help, whom God himself considered indispensable to his Incarnation, and whom the Catholic and Orthodox churches, following his lead, consider indispensable to the fullness of the faith. Most Anglo-Catholic and Greek Orthodox priests would accept the Marian beliefs, though many would say that acceptance of them was not necessary to salvation.

If Protestants are correct in believing that the dogmas of Mary's immaculate conception and bodily assumption are only pious imagination, unsubstantiated by Scripture, early tradition, or sound reason—then, of course, they can legitimately continue to ignore the universal influence of Our Blessed Mother. But I would guess that few of those who so vociferously scorn these beliefs ("How soon will His Holiness declare that the ass in the stable at Bethlehem was assumed into heaven?") have ever bothered to make a personal study of the historical tradition involved. Most Protestants take their faith from one pope or another, so that when a humanist preacher assures them that all men are sinless, or when a professor laughs over the absurdity of thinking that any particular man could actually have been God in the flesh, then the poor authority-ridden "freethinkers" fall into line without a whimper or a why. More dangerous still are the saintly heretics whose exemplary lives and loving concern for their flocks do more than mere words to spread the infection of their false convictions.

The truth is that none of us is clever enough or holy enough to make up a faith. We mostly take it from someone else, from true disciple or false prophet, from God or the Devil. The tragedy is that we do not always insist upon seeing the credentials of those who claim to be God's ambassadors.

Christ in Fragments?   16 August 1954

Everywhere there is talk about "our unity in Christ and our disunity as churches." At the opening plenary session Dr. Edmund Schlink confessed: "We are filled with shame that through our disunity we deny the unity of the body of Christ, and so make it quite easy for the world to cast aside the message that

Christ is its only hope." At the second plenary session, Dr. Visser 't Hooft said that the World Council of Churches desires "*manifest* unity, unity which is not merely invisible but tangible and concrete. For it is only by the manifestation of oneness that, as our Lord prayed, the world can come to believe."

He said that the real motive of the ecumenical movement was this: "Let the Church be the Church as it was intended to be by its Lord." But what did Christ intend his Church to be? That is the bone of contention.

The colorful processionals and solemn pageantry of this Assembly have been carefully planned to produce and encourage a feeling of unity among the representatives of our fragmented Christendom. Except among the Anglo-Catholics and Greek Orthodox, the general belief is that historical Church unity, which once existed in its fullness, has been lost and must be recaptured. This alleged loss of unity is blamed by theologians on man's inescapable sinfulness, which God supposedly could not counteract without violating man's freedom.

But is this not foolishness and absurdity to say that the Church has been shattered into fragments? It is the Mystical Body of Christ: is Christ, then, divided? And if Christ is indivisible, how could the unity of the Church have ever been lost?

The New Testament speaks only of a visible Church, the Body through which the Spirit of the risen and glorified Lord now operates in this world. It tells us that this Church, or kingdom, will include wheat and tares, good and bad fish, wise and foolish bridesmaids. In spite of this admixture of evil, Jesus Christ promises to be with it all days. He says that his own Holy Spirit will lead it into all truth. Manifest unity is of the essence in this New Testament picture of the Church.

It would, therefore, seem impossible, granted the deity of Jesus Christ and the reliability of the gospel record, that God should not have preserved this Church in oneness and true doctrine through the historical actuality of a visible society.

But perhaps this reasoning is fallacious. At least the rejoinder is often made that divisions have always existed, that even St. Paul was shocked by the contending parties he found at Corinth. But these divisions, it can be answered, did not result in the setting up of myriad schismatic communions. St. Augustine contends that this is the greatest sin, to set up altar against altar and dismember the Body of Christ.

It is a salutary sign that contrition for the sin of such denomi-nationalism is strong and sincere at this Evanston Assembly. No matter who is right and who is wrong on the basic issues in-volved, it is a good thing that all are saying: "Let the Church be the Church as it was intended to be by its Lord."

But what did Christ intend his Church to be? May the Holy Spirit of truth lead my mind aright on this question. May God's wisdom give me sure and certain enlightenment. So may I do his will and not my own.

Ut Omnes Unum Sint   18 August 1954

The crowds at the fifth plenary session sang out with gusto: "His chariots of wrath the deep thunderclouds form/ And dark is his path on the wings of the storm."

Two of the last three mornings I have been wakened by a cacophony of heavy rainfall interspersed with ear-splitting drum-beats of thunder. This morning once again the heavens have opened and are sending down a watery deluge. We have seen an unaccountable gathering of storm clouds over Evanston since the beginning of the Assembly. And many of them seem to have gathered about the head of a questionable Hungarian bishop.

Bishop John Peter of Hungary, who sits in a Communist legis-lature and whom Hungarian refugees have denounced as a secret police agent, declared yesterday that although his church was state subsidized, it was given complete freedom of worship. To the question: "Are you permitted to hold mass meetings outside of the churches?" he replied: "I am sorry for it, but it is permitted. Roman Catholic processions to the traditional places are so large that you could not imagine it. That is why I say I am sorry for it." This tongue-in-cheek answer was greeted by an appreciative ripple of laughter.

Dr. Toyohiko Kagawa, Japan's best-known living saint, when asked how Christians in Japan reacted to the American H-bomb experiments, replied: "Not only Christians, but all Japanese say if you want to experiment with H-bombs, do it in Alaska." Radio-active particles so filled the atmosphere after the South Pacific explosions that food exposed to the air was dangerous to eat.

Bishop Anders Nygren of Sweden told the fifth plenary session: "When the 'churches' meet together, their point of depar-ture must not lie in a discussion of external things but must be precisely this question: 'What is the Church essentially, i.e., in its indissoluble union with Christ himself?' " Bishop Nygren maintained that "the Church of Christ is already a unity . . . The prayer of Jesus for the unity of his Church has already been heard by the Father." For Jesus not only prayed "that they may all be one" (John 17:21), but he also affirmed: "Father, I thank thee that thou hast heard me. I knew that thou hearest me always" (John 11:41–42).

Canon Oliver Tomkins, warden of an Anglican theological school, candidly admitted: "We do not agree on the nature of the unity God wills for us . . . but in some sense the church is one . . . and we have an obligation to manifest that unity."

Dr. Charles Malik, Lebanon's ambassador to the United States, underlined the disastrous results which four-and-a half centuries of Protestant disunity have had upon Western civilization, when he said to the seventh plenary session: "At the present rate of spiritual impotence, hidden by the protective covering of the hy-drogen bomb, it is only a matter of time before the whole of Asia and Africa, and maybe even Europe, will be engulfed by Communism."

Everyone here at Evanston seems to agree that, despite the terrifying urgency of our times, no workable plan of organic Christian union can be expected to emerge among the member churches for many a decade. But time is running out, and our tragically divided world cannot afford to wait.

Is it wise, then, to place our hope in these fragmented sects and schismatic communions? Christ himself is the only hope of the world, but he works through his Mystical Body, which from earliest times has been called "the One Holy, Catholic and Apostolic Church." Can these 161 "churches" really be that ever-so-durable kingdom (Dan. 2:44; Luke 1:33) which Our Divine Lord founded and promised to guide by his own Holy Spirit? Can the Holy Spirit contradict himself in essential teachings, producing division upon division? Is Christ himself, then, divided?

As I think these dangerous thoughts, I feel like the child in Hans Christian Andersen's fable *The Emperor's New Clothes*. Here amid this pageantry they are saying: "It may not look it, but we are really one and must manifest this unity." In the fable, as the parade passed, they said: "What a marvelous suit of clothes the king is wearing!" I am afraid that I am no more impressed by theologians' talk of our wonderful eschatological unity than the fabled child by the king's stark nakedness. The awful truth of Evanston strikes me personally as being simply this: "We have nothing on at all!"

Intelligence and Courage   26 August 1954

Looking back through personal letters and papers of a bygone decade, I have come across a poem of mine printed in Italy in a book of verse by members of the British Eighth Army. Though I had little interest in religion at that time, the vaguely Christian humanitarianism I espoused paid full honor to the virtues of intelligence and courage, which now I need so desperately. In a sense, Ulysses is early archetypal man striving to deal with destiny.

ULYSSES

What use is boldness to the palsied hand
Or wisdom to the will that learns too late?
The man who does not early counter fate,
Submitting self to heaven's dread demand,
Is lost; nor can the learnèd fool withstand
The siren cries that never once abate,
Deny destruction's nymphs that lie in wait
On many a languid strip of yellow sand.
Then bind me now by reason's strongest cord
And pay no heed to my most longing plea:
Oh let the ship be swift and surely oared
And run up all the canvas full and free:
For we must sail through waters unexplored
And journey past the perils of the sea.[41]

Counting the Cost   27 August 1954

I was surprised and pleased to learn by long-distance telephone that in our absence and without our knowledge a Church Council Meeting was held at which our salary was given its second raise this year. This brings us, if rent value of the recently renovated parsonage be included, to a comfortable monthly sum.

And we do love our parsonage. It's a cozy and compact Cape Cod type house, our first home after a series of third floor apartments during theological school days. Even its slanting floors and settling foundations have become dear to us. Originally a tavern and stagecoach stopover, it was a halfway house between New York and Boston. Perhaps it is a halfway house for us too. At any rate, the old bar-room has become a minister's study. A cross on a bookcase has taken the place of the whiskey bottle on the bar. There has been a change of spirits.

We love our church too. Downstairs in the library room there are many small chairs for the children. We expect almost two hundred to register for the Sunday School this year. Upstairs in the sanctuary the benches are a chaste white, the carpeting a warm maroon, and the ceiling a soft blue. On the rear wall there is a bronze plaque listing twelve of the church's fourteen ministers, the first two of whom covered a century between them! The second, Shubael Bartlett, is an ancestor of a Yale '43 classmate who somehow was born into a Roman Catholic family. The church choir gathers in front of the bronze plaque before it processes down the north aisle each Sunday morning. Later they sing like angels at my back, for the pulpit is high and central, and the choir is grouped behind the minister's chair on either side of the organ. Before the pulpit is the communion table at which the four deacons and I have officiated so many times.

I must be sure and double sure before making any move on the Roman Catholic question. My decision cannot be impulsive. It must be time-tested and time-matured. There is also the difficult and inevitable loss of friendships involved. And extremely important, the effect of it all on the molding of our children's personalities.

When in doubt, go slowly. There is no recrossing the bridges of the past once they have been burned.

Come Home   28 August 1954

I have been greatly moved this evening by an account of how the weak and indecisive Gregory XI returned to Rome,[42] ending the Babylonian captivity of the papacy. St. Catherine of Siena never tired of demanding this Pope's return in fulfillment of his secret vow.[43] She begged him to ignore the plea of selfish relatives and black sheep cardinals that he remain in Avignon. She cried aloud for manly courage: "I beg you from Christ crucified that it may please Your Holiness to act promptly. The more quickly you do it, the less you will suffer. . . ."[44]

As I read this account, I remembered that outside the downtown Methodist Church at Evanston, during the opening wor-

ship service of the World Council, a man carried a placard which
read: "All roads lead to Rome—come home."

Beginning Anew   1 September 1954

Almighty Creator, Ruler of both time and eternity, grant us
wisdom, that we may use the quickly spent treasure of this life
for your glory and our own lasting good. You have given us help
in the past and hope for the future, and so, O Lord, we look
to you in the present moment, acknowledging you are both the
light of this world and the King of eternal glory, our only help,
our only hope, forever and ever. Amen.

Here begins the fourth year of our first (and only?) pastorate.
The future is in God's hands.

Everlasting Father, the same yesterday, today, and forever, we
know that our life upon this earth is but a moment in the vast-
ness of eternity. In this precious and fleeting moment may we
firmly grasp the outstretched hand of your mercy, who with the
Son and the Holy Spirit lives and reigns ever, one God, world
without end. Amen.

Apostolic Tradition   4 September 1954

Truncated Protestants, who throw the Bible and early Church
practice overboard when these disagree with their preconceived
notions, nevertheless are seen to be nodding their heads affirma-
tively whenever the proposition is set forward that "the Bible is
our only rule of faith and practice," or as the Articles of Religion
in the *Book of Common Prayer* express it:

> Holy Scripture containeth all things necessary to salvation: so that
> whatsoever is not read therein, nor may be proved thereby, is not
> to be required of any man that it should be believed as an article
> of the Faith, or be thought requisite or necessary to salvation.

Now Holy Scripture itself contradicts this position. St. Paul
writes to a congregation that it must also hold to the teachings
which he did not write down: "So then, brethren, stand firm and

hold to the traditions which you were taught by us, either by word of mouth or by letter" (2 Thess. 2:15). He tells Timothy to "Follow the pattern of the sound words which you have heard from me . . . and what you have *heard* from me before many witnesses entrust to faithful men who will be able to *teach others also.*" (2 Tim. 1:13; 2:2, emphasis added).

Much apostolic teaching not recorded explicitly in the New Testament joined the *written* tradition at a later date through the creeds and pronouncements of the early Councils and in the writings of the first five centuries of Church Fathers and Doctors. Had the Christian truths never been set in writing, however, we should still have them by word of mouth, as did the first Christians. Oral tradition only *seems* to disappear under the influence of the written word.

Many of these Roman traditions Protestants today blithely accept without a qualm of conscience, such as Catholic liturgy and creeds, the reliability and inspired character of Scripture, the observance of Sunday, Advent, Lent, and the feasts of Christmas, Easter, and Pentecost. Inconsistently, however, they discard other essential portions of Biblical revelation and early Church practice, such as personal confession to a priest, the real and actual presence of God in the Eucharist, the primacy of Peter and his successors.

This presumption of picking and choosing among the gems of the faith—is it not the hallmark of heresy?

Tomorrow   13 September 1954

Tomorrow is the third birthday of our eldest child, Margaret Olivia. A cousin's large three-wheeler, carefully repainted in a soft pastel blue, is to be her surprise present, while her own smaller tricycle will be given to her sister, Mary Elizabeth.

How I wish I could speak with the young women Margaret and Mary will some day be! Instead, they play on the floor with their toys or sleep in their cribs upstairs, completely ignorant of their father's struggle to find God's truth. Some day when they are grown up, and as lovely as their guardian angels, they may read these words, and with the latter's help, they may understand why their childhood in this garden spot—with its contented farm animals, companion children, and good Protestant people—had to be cut short.

For sooner or later the season of indecision will pass. Even now I am ninety-eight percent intellectually convinced that Rome is right, that disunion and disintegration is the only alternative for our civilization and our souls.

Tomorrow? Some resolution of the mind, some ray of revelation, some opening door of opportunity may draw my faltering steps into the next room. God's hidden grace works behind such things. " . . . at some moment, in answer to my prayers, the point of departure must come, as it comes between sleep and wakefulness when you find yourself ready to get up."[45]

Pray for Us All   14 September 1954

Brother Francis, joyous poor man of Assisi, friend of the sun and the moon, of water, fire, and earth, you seem closer to the world of nature than the world of men. Like a child you delighted in the innocent goodness of the animal kingdom. You preached to the birds. You shared your beggar's meals with stray dogs. In a dry season you fed the dying bees with sweet wine and honey. You made a forty-day retreat in company with a hare on Isola Maggiore in Lago Trasimento, which I have visited.

You blessed the world of men by your presence, but you were also a lover of silence and solitude. You were a humble worker of hidden miracles. You knew how to be a child among children. You were a second Christ. At dawn on the festival of the Elevation of the Holy Cross, you received the marks of our Lord in your body—14 September 1224.

Now on this 730th anniversary of God's gift to you of his own stigmata—O brother Francis, pray for a little child who is but three years old this day. Pray for Margaret—and for her sister Mary, who was born on the saint's day of Francis de Sales. Pray for us all. Through the unity of the communion of saints in Jesus Christ our Lord. Amen.

Study the Saints 16 September 1954

Francis Bernadone and Francis de Sales, Francis Xavier and Ignatius Loyola, Thomas Aquinas and Thomas More, Theresa de Cepeda and Juan de Yepes, Catherine Labouré and Bernadette Soubirous—is it not a happy thought to believe that these glorious saints are really our brothers and sisters? It should be a merry thought, for as one of them said: "A sad saint would be a sorry saint!"

The ties which bind a Catholic to the communion of saints, and make him one family with the great mystics and miracle-workers of God, are stronger than the ties of flesh and blood. Here in these holy men and women is a kinship, an example, an attractive vision and hope which earth cannot offer. Here once again for all to see stands the Christ, but in the common dress of our feeble humanity. Luther tried to sweep heaven clean of the saints: he failed. In 1522 he had seen truth when he said:

> When in his frailty a man invokes the saints, he invokes Christ, and without fail he will reach Christ whenever he calls upon their names, for wherever they are, they are in Christ and Christ in them, and their name in Christ's name and Christ's name in their name.[46]

The saints shine as the brightness of the firmament. They turn many to righteousness. They are as the stars for ever and ever. What right have Protestants to put out these lights when our Lord has commanded: "Let your light so shine before men, that they may see your good works and give glory to your Father who is in heaven?" (Matt. 5:16). Nowhere is the barren, friendless quality of the Protestant heaven more clearly seen than in this denial of fellowship with those who have gone before. It is a denial of the social character of religion. But the isolated individual cannot meet God divorced from his brothers, whether here or beyond. "A social being requires a social religion."[47] This is why the Church is a communion of saints, a solidarity. It is interknit and joined together by a single Spirit. It is the Mystical Body of Christ, "because we are members of his body" (Eph. 5:30). What therefore God has joined together, let not unbelief put asunder.

The Council of Trent defends this marriage of true minds, and it assures us of the help which sinners can gain through the communion of saints, when it states definitively:

> The saints, who reign together with Christ, offer up their own prayers to God for men. It is good and useful suppliantly to invoke them, and to have recourse to their prayers, aid and help for obtaining benefits from God, through his Son Jesus Christ, who alone is our Redeemer and Savior. Those persons think impiously who deny that the saints, who enjoy eternal happiness in heaven, are to be invoked; who assert that they do not pray for men. . . .[48]

To the potential convert, hesitating on the threshold of aggressive inquiry and regular instruction, no better advice could be given, I believe, than this: study the saints. For a start, read such books as *Great Saints*, by Walter Nigg, a Swiss Protestant, or *Saints Are Not Sad*, a recent Catholic anthology. Then get down to longer individual biographies. Study the way of the lowly. Live with the lessons they teach. Enter into their spirit of godly joy. Rest in their radiance. Share in their sorrows. Seek their prayers.

This road I have followed for several years, albeit with slow and unsure step. The Franciscan lineage has held a special fascination for me ever since the penitent Poverello first stepped into our classroom during one of Dr. Bainton's spellbinding lectures at the Yale Divinity School. During World War II, I had the pleasure of visiting Assisi. The body of St. Clare, glass-encased, both repelled and fascinated me. Last year by overseas mail I requested the prayers of the Capuchin stigmatist, Padre Pio di Pietrelcina. Between trains in New York City, I have enjoyed many happy visits to the Franciscan Church near Pennsylvania Station. Our daughter Margaret Olivia was born on the anniversary of the stigmatization of St. Francis of Assisi. Mary Elizabeth was born on the calendar day which honors St. Francis de Sales. It would seem that in Christ the Poverello has sought to share with a poor and needy sinner some of his untold riches. But this is not to be wondered at—it is the custom of the saints!

Defending the Bible   20 September 1954

It is strange indeed how in modern times the Roman Catholic Church has at last begun to appear in her real light, that is, as the defender and champion of Holy Scripture; while some Protestant sects, which seemingly based their revolt on Bible truth, have become its desecrators. Modernist skeptics have denuded the Holy Book of its supernatural qualities to such an extent that many liberal Protestants, when they do not utterly ignore it, consider the Bible as a merely human hodgepodge of folklore and forgeries, legends and myths, subjective imaginations and vain verbosities. Fundamentalists, at the other extreme, harden their interpretation into a narrow-minded literalism, which cannot survive the attacks of genuine scientific scholarship.

The skeptical modernist critics are the more devastating. By destroying popular faith in the inerrancy of the Holy Book, they have helped to undermine our objective Christian morality, which has been based on the common acceptance of Biblical authority. The skeptical spirit of this "rationalist" criticism has hacked away the armor of faith piece by piece and text by text. Biased against anything even remotely supernatural, many of these modernists reject the Incarnation and the miracles of God the Son as incongruous to their own preconceived notions and therefore inadmissible. They are enamored of the myth of Biblical myth. The portrait of our Lord in the gospels, they believe, was fabricated by the early Church to suit its apologetic needs. How convenient to classify as a "later addition" any and all parts of Scripture which disagree with one's long-nursed heretical misjudgments! And how satisfying to do it so rationally and so objectively!

The fact is that in the early centuries the One Original Church selected from the myriad "sacred" books those that were really inspired by God. God had moved their authors to write, giving them free rein of personal expression but preventing them from falling into error. These works the Church included in the New Testament and declared them authentic. She who mothered and produced them in the first place continued down the centuries to reproduce in her monasteries copies for distribution. Her authority pronounced upon the accuracy of properly translated versions and condemned as harmful translations purveying error. The New Testament is thus, in all truth, a Catholic production and a Catholic property. It would seem logical that this same Church alone should have God-given authority of interpretation and textual criticism. Heretical scholars are really trespassing upon another's domain, though usually in all good conscience since they do not see it in this light.

How desperately authoritative interpretation is needed can readily be seen from the mass of conflicting meanings which have been derived by Protestant sects from the simple words "This is my Body." The Bible is full of obscurities: its meaning is not always obvious, even to the spiritually-minded and scholarly. What then of the worldly and ignorant? Who is to lead them into right understanding? Did our Lord not die for them, too?

Not only is the Bible partially obscure, but it does not tell the whole story. Only a portion of the original deposit of faith has here been recorded. As John tells us, if all the things done by our Lord had to be written down, "that the world itself could not contain the books that would be written" (John 21:25). The Bible alone is decidedly not sufficient unto salvation: apostolic tradition must supplement and surround the scriptural witness. And how are we to be sure of the truth of either unless the claim of the Roman Catholic Church to be guaranteed by Christ in giving them to us is valid? The Vatican Council of 1870 issued the following statement:

> The Church considers the books of the Bible sacred and canonical, not because they were composed only by human industry and af-

terwards approved by her authority, nor only because they contain revelation without error, but because, written under the inspiration of the Holy Ghost, they have God as their author and as such have been committed to the Church.[49]

Dark Horse   21 September 1954

God has instituted law and order among men for the restraint of evil and the benefit of society. All Christians, therefore, have a sacred duty to help foster good government through the political party of their choice.

My own scanty political activity having caught up with me, I was unexpectedly nominated last night at the caucus to stand for Representative to the State Legislature. When they ran short of candidates, the local Episcopal minister suggested my name. This is a part-time, short-term job from January to June, which I will do as best I can, if elected, but I guess it means the end for a while of these *Threshold Thoughts*.

First Day of Autumn   23 September 1954

So ends a half year of keyhole-peeping into the mind of a potential Roman convert. We do not see very much of the dim interior, but what we do see is something highly scandalous! Or so it may seem to the provincial sort of unbeliever with his inbuilt restricted-span-of-vision. Of such a one, if he begin to question his sight, our Lord will ask: "What do you want me to do for you?" May he remember the divine warning: "If your eye is not sound, your whole body will be full of darkness. If then the light in you is darkness, how great is the darkness!" (Matt. 6:23). May he reply with the humility of the blind: "Master, let me receive my sight" (Mark 10:51).

Touch my eyes, O healing Christ, that I may see you. This night of uncertainty gives me no rest. Lead me, then, into the noonday fullness of your truth. And lest I stumble at the sudden splendor, O strong Companion, take my hand. Amen.

Providential Defeat?   2 November 1954

After a hard-fought campaign and a close race, the opposition candidates, God bless them, were all elected. We came out ahead on one side of town but lost by a greater margin on the other side.

So it's back to my free-time Catholic considerations again with no more political postponements!

Marian Doctrines   8 November 1954

Many Protestants have a wrong attitude toward Our Lady because they hold inadequate beliefs about Our Lord. The Church itself did not really begin to see Mary in her full light until the problems about her Son had been cleared up. It took half a millennium to settle those many problems about his two natures, divine and human, which were raised by Sabellius, Arius, Nestorius, Eutyches, Sergius, and other early heretics. This is why the greatest Marian doctrines did not begin to appear explicitly until the fifth and sixth centuries. They were contained in the doctrines about her Son and could be seen clearly only after those were seen.

Truth Is One   9 November 1954

It is fatal to look at the Roman faith as a series of chopped-up doctrines. Truth is one at the central inner core and must be seen as a single organism to be rightly known. However necessary it may be to consider Catholic teachings individually, it is the relation which each bears to the whole which makes them all hold together and make sense. Dissecting the members of a corpse will not give an understanding of the living, moving person. No more can the accumulated understanding of isolated dogmas make one a Catholic. God must draw the soul to the center that is Christ, from whose splendorous light radiate the many seemingly separate beams of truth.

Keeping in Contact   12 November 1954

Yesterday afternoon at the Catholic Lending Library in Hartford, where the two young clerks were as happy and helpful as ever, I saw a poster announcing a Family Life Conference and Cana Institute at which a lay theologian whom I had long wished to meet was to be the lead-off speaker. I left the bookstore with Butler's *Church and Infallibility* and Prescott's *Jerusalem Journey* under my arm, and in my head the firm purpose of attending that Catholic gathering.

The lay theologian, Frank Sheed, had a delightful sense of humor. In discussing the moral law he assured his audience that God does not look down from heaven and say: "Men seem to be enjoying themselves. What can I stop?" The moral law is simply God's sure advice on the best way to run our lives.

I had a chat with this British theologian after his talk, and he graciously suggested that we lunch together in New York next Friday. This will be a joy for me, since for some time I have respected his books and sensed that I might find in him a wise spiritual father.

Tomorrow my wife will attend a session of the Family Life Conference. A nun who runs a nursery and teaches child psychology at St. Joseph College in West Hartford will be the speaker. Let us hope she will chalk up one more mark for the Catholic Church in my wife's undecided mind! At least she seems eager to attend.

Marjorie has always been interested in the effect of religious vows upon the individual. On the street she peeps at the face under each starched white wimple, trying to see if convent life brings the peace and joy of God or the frustrations hinted at by anti-Catholics. Whether she would admit it or not, she is really impressed by these dedicated lives. Perhaps the nun whom she will hear tomorrow afternoon will deepen that impression.

In the Catholic Church there is a breadth and depth of religious experience that Protestantism does not offer. This was brought home to my wife a few years ago by some experiences she had in Germany, where she worked with displaced persons. Church World Service stationed her at Ulm on the Danube. There she attended most often an ancient, partially-bombed Catholic church, because it had a "prayed-in feeling." The Reformation-stripped Lutheran cathedral she found to be outwardly magnificent but inwardly barren. Since she could follow neither the Latin of the Roman mass, nor the rapid German oratory of the Lutheran sermon, she chose the church where she sensed the fuller presence of the Holy Spirit. While in Ulm, she also enjoyed visiting the nearby Cloisters of Blaubeuren, whose gothic chapel, lovingly wrought by the hands of the monks, was of exquisite and enduring beauty.

Marjorie also came into contact with Bavarian Catholicism in other, more personal ways. Of the two young German women she most admired, the one, a prominent anti-Nazi whose brother and sister had been hanged by Hitler as a warning to the students of Munich, became a Catholic convert soon after the war, while the other, less illustrious but equally unswayed by the perverted propaganda of the Nazi masterminds, wrote to us last spring of her own conversion. Such varied pasts and paths can lead to Rome!

Better Half   22 November 1954

For some time now my wife and I have carried on sporadic conversations about Roman Catholic motives of credibility. Marjorie has not as yet read this journal, though of course she knows I am writing it. I'll show it to her when I get it typed up. Naturally I hope and pray that God will give her the faith, so that what we do we can do together. Mixed marriages labor under too many burdens. Disagreements are bound to result where loyalties are divided, and it is generally the children who suffer the most.

The better half of our team is a well-integrated, naturally good person, if there ever could be one. Her disposition, quite unlike mine, is almost ceaselessly celestial. She has imperfections, to be sure, but they are few and far between. She contributes bountifully to the life of our present parish. The children and young people who benefit from her nondirective leadership will miss her greatly—if we leave, as I now feel certain that we shall. She has done them so much good just by being her quiet self in their company.

What could be more difficult than to convert this type of happy Protestant to the Catholic way of believing? Were she to remain a Protestant, she might easily get into heaven with a plea of invincible ignorance, for she has read few of the books about Catholicism which have been my steady diet. From her youth up she has inhaled the Protestant atmosphere. Indeed, there has been a Protestant minister in almost every generation of her mother's family since before the Revolutionary War. This generation would have seen a break in that line, if she herself had not—after graduation from Oberlin College and Yale Divinity School—been ordained into the ministry of the Congregational Church. On the fourteenth of June, 1951, we were jointly ordained in Marquand Chapel at Yale University. My oldest brother, who is also a Congregational minister and the headmaster of a small preparatory school, took part in the service.

The barrier of bad Catholics[50] will be difficult for Marjorie to breach. Only the opposite example of the saints could help her do it. Like many other potential converts, she has been acquainted with some of those professing Catholics whose lives have fallen far short of even the most lax Protestant standards. Thank goodness she prays regularly and can act upon God's guidance when it comes to her! Thank goodness the saints appeal to her! Theology does not. But there are many roads, and it would seem that God in his inscrutable way is drawing Marjorie along her own particular path.

May his supernatural life within her soul guide her surely! May he in whom there is no darkness call her into the light of his own true Church—which in spite of the tares is holy, because its Founder, doctrine, sacraments and saints are pure and holy beyond compare.

Clean Hands   24 November 1954

Margaret and Mary have taken to praying for us at bedtime in the same way as we pray for them. Religious pictures, hung high beyond their reach, decorate the walls of their rooms. Holding them up in my arms, I take both girls on a tour of these sights before putting them to bed. Then the blankets have to be arranged just right, the big stuffed dogs put in place, and the favorite picture books made available. Once the prayers have begun, they are difficult to stop. Indeed, they should go on and on as long as possible, because the longer the prayer, the longer Daddy will stay in the room.

At the table, also, they fold their hands and sing a grace: "Thank him, thank him,/ All ye little children—/ God is love, God is love." Mary, not yet two, has been heard to mumble on afterward about blessing us and all our relatives.

Margaret arrived in this world just three weeks after we arrived in this parish. She was three in September and is getting to be quite an adult lady. Sometimes she will place a hand on my head and say a prayer her mother taught her: "God bless Daddy, and keep him safe and well and happy and good. Amen." I close my eyes and let the little saint work, thinking that surely Jesus must hear such prayers and answer them. Then I begin to wonder what long-range plans he may have for these two children within the ongoing life of the Catholic Church.

Feast of the Immaculate Conception   8 December 1954

A man needs to know where he's going in life and how to get there. The seven sacraments, along with prayer and obedience, are the divinely ordained way to man's final goal, which is union with God.

Such threshold thoughts as these went through my mind as I entered St. Joseph's Cathedral this afternoon. I remembered, too, the Archbishop's service of solemn installation, which I had attended a year ago this fall—with its stately procession of priests in white surplices, the reverential throngs, the high dignitaries,

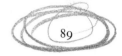

the glimmering candles, the strange incense, and the red-robed Christ agleam in his central window above the high altar.

The Cathedral was empty. I knelt in a pew down front, and for the first time in my life, hesitatingly but with joy, I said the rosary. The beads I held, as I meditated upon the five glorious mysteries, had been given me at that papal audience a decade ago this last June, shortly after the fall of Rome to the Allied Armies. I had only recently removed them from my cache of Italian souvenirs. Eugenio Pacelli, His Holiness Pope Pius XII, had blessed them, and the intention now of their first use was his strengthening and recovery of health, if such be the will of Almighty God. At death's door, he has been confined to his bed for a week. Today he was unable to take full part in the rites which closed the Marian Year. He assisted at a Mass in his room. His voice, transmitted from the sickbed by loudspeaker, imparted an Apostolic Blessing to hushed thousands who kept vigil in St. Peter's Square and around the Basilica of St. Mary Major.

May the divine assistance remain always with him. And when at last he is called up higher, may the Sacred College of Cardinals elect once again an able and conscientious successor in that never-failing line of those who have followed the Big Fisherman as Servant of the Servants of God.

Crossing the Threshold   9 December 1954

A little over a week ago—with a delicious feeling of release and a prayer of thanks to my Creator—I finished writing the last chapter in *Catholicism or Chaos*, part two of this poor man's apologia. In making this objective carving of Roman doctrine I have come to understand more fully many of the beliefs that gave me difficulty. If I have failed to show a proper spirit of charity in its composition, may God and my Protestant friends forgive me. I have tried to be as kind as honesty would permit. As for the enemies this book will make if it is ever published (John 15:19; Luke 6:22), may the Lord bless each and every one of them, as the evangelist Billy Graham would say, "real good."

"And now, behold," Paul said to the elders of Ephesus, "I am going to Jerusalem, bound in the spirit, not knowing what shall befall me there" (Acts 20:22). For a long time now, I have believed that whatever God, our supreme good, tells us must unquestionably be true, because he cannot deceive. This is faith, and it is God who produces this attitude in the soul. He also moved my will to seek out the authentic human teacher of revealed truth, that I might know with certainty all the things he has said. I now believe that the Roman Catholic Church teaches absolute truth by the authority of the living God. To this truth I must therefore submit my life and my destiny. I have reached this decision through personal study and prayer, and I thank the many Catholic authors I have read for the enlightenment received from their books. I have not fallen under the spell of any powerful human personality or moving evangelical experience. God himself through his Spirit and his Church has fed the burning hunger for truth which he long ago kindled in my soul.

There must be a further short period of waiting—just to be sure I'm sure—but then the bridges will have to be burned and that unique, little-known land explored. For the sake of my wife and children may God guide me aright in this difficult adventure. If my mind is not playing tricks on me, and this new-found faith does not disappear like a bubble into the air before, let us say, next Easter, then I shall take my stand publicly. An irrevocable destiny-decision should not be hurried: it must be time-tested and time-matured.

No one can judge another's conscience. Each man brings himself to judgment by the decisions he makes. My own mind and will have come under captivity to the *whole* Word of God. And this book is witness thereto. Small as I am—"here I stand. I cannot do otherwise. God help me. Amen."[51]

PART TWO

CATHOLICISM OR CHAOS

I

Test All Things Afresh

"A twig can be cut with a bread knife, but an oak calls for an ax." So said Martin Luther, the strong Saxon woodsman, as he cut mightily into the hardwood trunk of medieval Catholicism.

The cry "timber" has never gone up. The tree has never come down. Generation by generation the axes grow duller, the axmen weaker. Branches, it is true, have been lopped off in many sizes and at all stages of growth. But their greenery somehow fades and their bark cracks, as if they might soon be gathered up and cast into the fire.

The oak still stands. The Saxon woodsman marked it as a tree of death, whose high pretensions the Lord of heaven and earth would soon bring crashing downward. Its defenders called it the tree of life, whose leaves were meant for the healing of the nations.

The nations of Western civilization have undergone a ghastly spiritual impoverishment since the time of the Protestant Reformation. The disease of secularism is far more virulent today than it ever was in the sixteenth century. Modern man has capitulated almost completely to the exclusive practicality of the here and now. He has lost the sense of God's presence. A restless uneasiness has seized his soul. Believing himself to be no more than a particle of meaningless matter, he has tried with frantic zeal to dissolve his loneliness in one collective fanaticism after another. More and more he becomes a hollow man, belonging nowhere, fury-driven by the demons of ceaseless anxiety and nameless guilt, which rise up from the abyss of his own nothingness.

The world no longer believes because it no longer hears One voice. The cries of conflicting sects, divided doctrinally, have closed its ears to the truth. The Body of Christ has been drawn and quartered, clawed and torn into hundreds of separate pieces. And this is how the Church has been re-formed.

The Church was in dire need of a moral reformation at the beginning of the sixteenth century. While Luther was growing up at Mansfeld and studying at Erfurt, a profligate pope, whose worldliness and nepotism were brazened before all, was followed by a power-hungry one who preferred politics to reform, and he in his turn by a hedonist. Of this latter pope, a Medici, it is written: "His court, with its lavish expenditure on wholly secular objects, the card-table, the theatre, the chase, stood in sharp contradiction to the aims and calling of a great dignitary of the Church."[52]

Such luxury was expensive, and for its support heavy taxes were levied in the non-Italian branches of the Church. Financial abuses flourished, simony was widespread, malfeasance in high office was all too common, and many monasteries were polluted by an excess of the humanist spirit. Pagan attitudes and vices ran wild. Religious devotion was at the nadir.

Such moral corruption accounts for much of the Reformation's success among the people, but not for Luther's own revolt, which was doctrinal. It was against self-justification and the belief in good works as meritorious that he first took his stand. Early sixteenth-century scandals did not change the essence of the Church, nor the purity of her teachings on faith and morals. But it was against these basic teachings that Luther rebelled. As one of the most colorful and scholarly pens in Protestantism has put it:

> Luther's initial cry was not a castigation of the crew. It was the ship to which he objected. "Others," said he, "have attacked the life. I attack the doctrine." Not the abuses of medieval Catholicism, but Catholicism itself as an abuse of the Gospel was the object of his onslaught.[53]

Was this doctrinal attack justified? In view of the growth of social and religious chaos during the last four centuries, in view too of the continuing growth of the tree to which he laid his axe, Luther himself[54] would surely wish to re-examine the work of destruction he initiated almost unwittingly. He would agree with the Lutheran minister in Germany who recently said: "We must test all things afresh and we ourselves must be tested by Scripture."[55]

Test all things afresh? Luther cannot do this. But we can and must.

2

Scrupulosity's Fruit

The Black Death, national grievances, corrupt clergy, fossilized scholasticism, secularizing humanism, and an exiled papacy—these provided the tinder wood of the Reformation. But the match that lit the blaze was scrupulosity. For Martin Luther and John Calvin both suffered from this dread disease of the soul.

Martin Luther early learned the resentment felt by children who suffer from harsh discipline. Parents and teachers taught him well the sting of the switch and the fear of punishment. He developed an inclination toward brooding and melancholy. Like the gothic cathedrals of his day, his soul aspired, exalted with soaring spiritual hopes, but only to be plummeted into the depths of emotional depression by the thought of God's implacable wrath and the terrors of hell. He pleaded with God for his very existence and hated him for his justice. "Thus I angrily rushed around in my bewildered conscience," he wrote. The tensions of deep-rooted fear made him dynamically subjective in all his considerations. This dark magnetism attracted to the core of his troubled personality only those truths adaptable to it: he lived in a microcosm of his own mind's making.

Luther at Erfurt was trained in the Pelagian nominalism of Occam, which taught that man by his own merits and the Church's sacramental help could achieve moral perfection, freedom from self-love and deceit. In reaction to this false optimism he swung to the opposite extreme of Augustinian pessimism as to man's nature and actions. Man was inherently corrupt, his will enslaved to sin and Satan. External means of grace, Luther eventually concluded, were of little use: they did not help his own inner distress. Man, being so evil, could not co-operate in his own salvation. All the credit for man's salvation must go to God. Humiliate man, glorify God—this became the first Protestant formula. Since in the arena of the soul God effected all the saving work directly, the visible Church with its secondary mediators and means of grace was almost unnecessary. How the world was to be Christianized did not trouble him; individual subjectivity was paramount. This emphasis, reached after years of inner storm and struggle, sprang from the original set of his soul.[56]

Passionate of nature, he was driven by an ever-deepening, irrational guilt of conscience into periods of intense despair. This *tentatio tristitiae*,[57] or dread concerning his sins, magnified guilt beyond all reality. Obsessed with such inner corruption, he went daily to confession. He tried beyond endurance his poor patient confessor, until he exclaimed: "Man, God is not angry with you. You are angry with God. Don't you know God commands you to hope?" The vicar of his order, one Johann von Staupitz, believed his charge to be suffering from "the scruples of a sick soul. 'Look here,' he said, 'if you expect Christ to forgive you, come in with something to forgive—parricide, blasphemy, adultery—instead of all these peccadilloes.' "[58]

Such was the make-up of the man who would eventually declare that all men were totally depraved through the corruption of original sin and that "the human will is not free but captive."

Luther tried everything to ease his disquieted conscience—the cowl, good works, mortification, saints and sacraments—all to no avail. So at last he gave up. The odds were all against him, he felt, and there was nothing he could do—except to believe and be made just through his faith! And yet this last resort provided no real purification here and now, but only "imputed" righteousness. According to this notion, Christ gives the sinner the robe of his own merits to cover his diseased and contaminated body: the robe is magnificent, but within it the man himself is unchanged.

Stricken with a somewhat milder case of scrupulosity was John Calvin, the son of an excommunicated Church attorney and treasurer. John Calvin was French to the core and logical to the point of heartlessness. He was classical, austere, and calm, though embittered against Catholic authority, which had censured both his father and his brother into social disrepute. Withdrawing to the protective hermitage of his studies, he became introspective and conscience-centered. He wrote: "The more I considered myself, the more my conscience was pricked with sharp darts, so much so that only one consolation remained and that was to deceive myself by forgetting about myself." But Calvin found no peace from his conviction of sin, until he found the doctrines of predestination and justification by faith. Then he cried out: "Only one haven of salvation is left for our souls, and that is the mercy of God in Christ. We are saved by grace—not by our merits, not by our works."

John Calvin and Martin Luther, each in his own way, suffered from that dread disease of the soul, scrupulosity. Sick souls inwardly troubled beyond measure, they longed for peace of mind, emotional assurance, subjective salvation.

Luther found this in a passage of Paul, which became for him the very gate to heaven: "a man is justified by faith" (Rom. 3:28). So deeply was he moved by this passage that he added to it, on his own authority, the word *alone*, forgetting that St. Paul had also said: "For in this hope we were saved" (Rom. 8:24), and "if I have all faith, so as to remove mountains, but have not love, I am nothing" (1 Cor. 13:2).

Calvin's own answer was his doctrine of absolute predestination, which agreed with Luther's dictum that "the human will is not free but captive." God has created innumerable slaves, the few elect for eternal joy, the majority of reprobates for the endless torments of hell. Omnipotence saves or damns arbitrarily from all eternity, and men can do nothing about it. Since "it is the Spirit himself bearing witness with our spirit that we are children of God" (Rom. 8:16), the elect "perceive" that they are saved hereafter, according to Calvin, just as they are "assured" of forgiveness here and now, according to Luther.

An Anglican comments as follows:

The doctrine of assurance is extremely dangerous, for "the heart is deceitful above all things" [Jer. 17:9], and the feelings are most untrustworthy guides . . . It is this doctrine of assurance which lies at the root of the individualism and subjectivity which are the bane of all the heirs of the Reformation. . . . If all that were needed for salvation were justification by faith, guaranteed by the assurance of a man's own heart, the Church would not be necessary; the sacraments would not be necessary; the observance of the moral law would not be necessary.[59]

Eventually these latter things are apt to seem secondary to the scrupulous, who become so enmeshed in their own subjective world-view that they lose their hold on objective reality. Peace of conscience becomes the chief aim of their lives. Truth falls by the wayside, a maimed, battered, and broken wreck.

The saints have always possessed sensitive and enlightened consciences. A sick and morbidly introspective conscience is an entirely different thing. With it, a person bogs down in the swamps of uncertainty, incessantly driven by doubts as to his guilt or innocence in this or that minor act. Weakened by sickness, fatigue, or nervous instability, the mind curves in upon itself, digs up the corruption of the past and feasts upon it. Solitary introspection becomes an opiate, self-concern a passion, self-condemnation a reverse pride. Such people are usually stubborn. They cling to their ill-founded fears like obstinate mules. They see the world as being filled with dangers and demons. No amount of reasoning avails. They are emotionally sick and often cannot help themselves.

Such a sufferer must first of all admit the incorrectness of his own conscience. Then he must substitute a correct conscience for his sick one. He is like a flyer whose compass has gone out of kilter: he is flying blind and must follow the radio beam in for a safe landing. The scrupulous modern Protestant is apt to seek this way out through identification with a psychological analyst or a ministerial counselor. Down the centuries scrupulous Catholics have been advised to select a compatible priest confessor and then obey him in all things. A spiritual director of some sort seems to be the only answer to such aberration.[60] It is true that Christ makes use of faith and truth to heal the sick soul; but he also uses doctors and directors, and most especially when chronic anxiety deprives the soul of the former spiritual gifts.

"If it had not been for Dr. Staupitz," Martin Luther said of his own confessor, "I should have sunk in hell."

Luther began to believe at this period that his many good works were doing him no good at all. Or as Calvin put it: "We are saved by grace—not by our merits, not by our works."

"Justification by Faith Alone" became the rallying cry of the Reformation. For "a man is not justified by works of the law but through faith in Jesus Christ" (Gal. 2:16), said Paul, and "a man is justified by faith apart from works of law" (Rom. 3:28).

Now St. Paul did not abrogate authority and obligation. But the Ten Commandments had been superseded by the law of charity: "love is the fulfilling of the law" (Rom. 13:10). In his lectures on *Galatians* Luther said this:

> We do not mean that the Law is bad. Only it is not able to justify us. To be at peace with God, we have need of a far better mediator than Moses or the Law. . . . I cannot be saved except by the blood and death of Christ. I conclude, therefore, that it is up to Christ to overcome my sins, and not up to the Law, or my own efforts.[61]

But does Christ overcome our sins merely by "imputing" a fictitious righteousness apart from any real sanctification and renovation of the soul? Or does he actually make the sinner just, and enable him to fulfill the law of love, which asks so much more of him than the Decalogue did, by imparting powers, gifts, and graces.

Our Lord said that he had come to fulfill the law and not to destroy it (Matt. 5:17), and he often urged the keeping of the Commandments (Matt. 19:17; John 14:15). He said that his disciples, being the light of the world, should let men see their good works (Matt. 5:16), which they could not do unless they abided in him (John 15:5) who had made them clean (John 15:3) and given them new life (John 5:21).

It would seem that Christ's master plan of salvation included the imparting of actual righteousness in order that the law of love might be kept and good works really done. This is why Catholicism teaches that in the justification of the sinner the merits of Christ's passion are here and now communicated to him by the Holy Spirit.

This means that when, in Christ's service and with the help of his grace, the believer does good works, these deeds are meritorious by virtue of the merit with which Christ supplies them. They will be rewarded not because of any inherent right but because Christ has promised to reward active charity (Matt. 25:31–46).

Such reward, of course, does not mean anything so crass as that we can "earn our way into heaven." Catholicism, contrary to much Protestant misinterpretation, teaches no such doctrine. All depends, in the last analysis and on the last day, upon the merits and mercy of the Savior of sinners.

Yet where grace-created merits do exist in sinners, they must be amply rewarded, as he promised they would be. Scripture bears constant witness to this doctrine of recompense for active charity. St. Paul, who is so often cited as teaching the single-formula heresy of "Justification by Faith Alone," tells us that God "will render to every man according to his works" (Rom. 2:6) and that "each shall receive his wages according to his labor" (1 Cor. 3:8). St. Peter warns us against being barren and unfruitful in Christ (2 Peter 1:8). And St. James says this: "What does it profit, my brethren, if a man says he has faith but has not works? Can his faith save him? . . . a man is justified by works and not by faith alone . . . for as the body apart from the spirit is dead, so faith apart from works is dead" (Jas. 2:14, 24, 26).

"When God crowns our merits," Augustine tells us in a clarifying sentence, "He crowns his own gifts" (*Epis.*, 194, 19). But Martin Luther the Augustinian never tired of denouncing the hope for reward from good works as a snare and a delusion. His own strenuous deeds had not availed to relieve the inner torture of his scrupulosity. He believed they would carry no more weight with God than they had with his own sick soul.

3

Revolt against Authority

To Georg Spalatin, humanist and priest, confidant of rulers and power at Court, in August 1520 Martin Luther said these words: "I am convinced that to destroy the papacy, all means are lawful to us." He would have been wiser to heed Thomas More's warning that if he and his supporters "denied the spiritual authority of the pope, they would remove the key stone of the arch that supported the order of society."[62]

Luther's rebellious words have been like a battle cry to the liberal religionists in their progressive revolt against authority. Subdividing their "churches" into countless bickering sects, they have asserted the supremacy of individualism to the point of anarchy. Consequently they have been "harassed and helpless, like sheep without a shepherd" (Matt. 9:36). The one force which has kept these centrifugal elements from flying to the four winds has been the passion of anti-Catholicism.[63] Shall an ambassador be sent to the head of the Roman Church? All Protestantism shouts with a single voice: "No!" Shall an ambassador be sent to the head of the Anglican Church? No protest is made, since fear of the papacy is not involved.

The anarchy of this excessive individualism—based upon a false persuasion of fundamental autonomy—has created a void of loyalties, an empty house into which have lately been rushing the seven evil spirits of absolute Caesarism. Statisms of the left and the right at least exercise a total claim upon the individual's life. He is promised regimentation and order in exchange for chaos and uncertainty, but at the price of surrendering his soul to a false god. Christianity, too, calls for total commitment, wholehearted devotion, but of this modern man is scarcely aware. He has been inoculated by small doses of weak, wizened faith against ever catching the real thing. He has never seen a saint, nor probably ever read the life of one. The type of Christian teaching he has heard from the hundreds upon hundreds of sects which fight for his attention has been, for the most part, a diluted, vague and ever-changing cluster of "opinions." The trumpets of Protestantism give forth uncertain sounds, and few prepare themselves for battle.

This is why Adolf Hitler, for example, was able to win so many German Protestants to his cause: he issued a hard if demonic challenge, a call to courage, commitment and self-renunciation. His contempt for those who were piously irrelevant and disorganized was well known. In a conversation with his intimates on April 7, 1933, he maligned the Protestant clergy as "insignificant little people, submissive as dogs, and they sweat with embarrassment when you talk to them. They have neither a religion they can take seriously nor a great position to defend like Rome."[64]

Though the slander of this judgment cannot be accepted by fair-minded men, still it contains a grain of truth. Protestantism has had no "great position." It has had hundreds upon hundreds of "great positions," one for each of the numberless sects which have proliferated by the principle of private judgment. The Pauline warning has been ignored: "I appeal to you, brethren, by the name of our Lord Jesus Christ, that all of you agree and that there be no dissensions among you, but that you be united in the same mind and the same judgement" (1 Cor. 1:10).

If Scripture may be interpreted by each individual according to his own lights, or by each group according to its own lights, a chaos of conflicting interpretations will result, and for each basic understanding a separate sect. If there were no Supreme Court to interpret the Constitution of the United States, but each individual were allowed to put such construction upon it as his measure of wisdom or honesty should suggest, what anarchy would result! What breakdown of civil society! But this is exactly the theory upon which Protestantism operates in the spiritual sphere, where it teaches that, since the Holy Spirit will immediately enlighten each reader, each may therefore make his own interpretation. St. Peter warned Christians against such private interpretation (2 Pet. 1:20), saying that there are verses in the Pauline epistles "which the ignorant and unstable twist to their own destruction, as they do the other scriptures" (2 Pet. 3:16).

Jesus Christ called for unity among his immediate followers and among those who should receive the faith through their word (John 17:20-21). He knew that the world would never learn anything from a babble of discordant witnesses. He established a teaching body and sent them to all nations to teach "all that I have commanded you" (Matt. 28:20). He gave them his own authority with the words: "As the Father has sent me, even so I send you" (John 20:21). Those who would learn of Christ must listen to these authorized spokesmen, whom a supernatural Power would keep in the truth (John 14:17, 26).

Now it is true that our Lord attacked the "blind guides" and "whited sepulchres" who exercised guiding authority over the Jews. However, it was not the principle or the office of authority which he impugned, but its misuse and abuse by hypocrites. "So practice and observe whatever they tell you, but not what they do; for they preach, but do not practice" (Matt. 23:3). He might utter these same words in connection with the occasional scandalous priest of our own day, condemning the man while upholding his office and valid teaching; for he fully guaranteed official Church doctrine against error when he said that the human apostolic voice was in reality his own infallible voice: "He who hears you hears me" (Luke 10:16). Through such dependable, incorruptible channels were God's people to receive his word.

Thus, and thus alone, was chaos to be conquered, according to the Founder of Christianity.

To one degree or another modern man has revolted against teaching authority in favor of divisive subjectivism. And this revolution has brought about a devaluation of man's reason, his highest faculty. It has sponsored an attack upon the reliability of the intellectual and logical processes. The first Renaissance re-action against medieval institutional authority turned man's pri-mary concern from God's eternal world to this temporal world, and in so doing it exalted man himself to the pivotal position formerly reserved for the Almighty. This enthronement of man at the center of all things led at first to the false glorification of his rational faculty. The limits of man's reason were not recog-nized, and the irrationality which now stalks our modern world in many guises is a reaction against this false deification of man and his reason, most especially against the enthronement of his mathematical and mechanical reason.

For half a millennium Western civilization has steadily turned from God to man, from spiritual realities to an obsession with material things and worldly gain. The glories of Gothic archi-tecture, of Gregorian plainsong, of Romanesque and Byzantine art—these at least pointed the medieval Christian soul toward heaven, and the song on his lips was often: "Glory to God in the highest!" Modern man has exchanged these masterpieces for the frenzy of jazz music, the immoral monstrosities of modern art, and the unimaginative ugliness of the squat factory building. What volumes of spiritual emptiness these inanities speak forth! They have resulted from a desire to enthrone human nature at the center of life, being and thought. The song on twentieth-century lips is apt to be: "Glory to man in the highest!"

The shattering truth is that man is completely dependent upon God, who has created him for his own glory. It is man's duty to live in obedience to God and his authorized representatives. But modern man will not accept his proper subordination any more than would his first progenitor, Adam.

Adam and Eve were the first human beings who refused to submit to God's authority. They were put to the test of obedi-ence through a prohibition: they were forbidden to eat the fruit of the tree of the knowledge of good and evil. But the serpent played upon their pride, and they revolted against God. This was the fall, their refusal to submit to God's authority.

Instead of punishing them as they deserved by death, God's

mercy merely deprived them of the preternatural gifts of integrity and the rest, and above all of sanctifying grace. Their children were henceforth born in a fallen condition, lacking original justice, ravaged by the downdrag of emotional disorder and lust. This unbalance was to produce further rebellion through pretensions of self-sufficient independence until the very end of time.

It called forth from the eternal realms the intervention of God the Son, who became man in order to right by humble obedience that which Adam had set under the curse of his proud disobedience. The supernatural goods lost through sin were returned to mankind through the suffering Messiah and the sacraments he instituted to fulfill his saving purpose. "If, because of one man's trespass, death reigned through that one man, much more will those who receive the abundance of grace and the free gift of righteousness reign in life through the one man Jesus Christ" (Rom. 5:17).

By one man's offense—blessing to Christians for ever and ever! *O felix culpa!* O happy fault! And yet, who is modern man, that he should repeat this offense of pride and revolt?

> What, then, is the radical sin of Western civilization? It is the great sin, the titanic, Promethean sin. It is the sin of believing and behaving as though man were an end in himself; as though humanity existed in its own right and for the sole purpose of its own glory and power.[65]

Philosophically speaking, man became an end in himself when the mathematical reason of Descartes, what Pascal called *l'esprit géométrique*, usurped the throne of metaphysics. His *cogito, ergo sum* shifted the emphasis from God's objective truth to egocentric certitude in a vain attempt to grant the human mind that intuitive knowledge which God has reserved to the angels.

This deification of man came to a head in the eighteenth-century Enlightenment, which endeavored to make reason the absolute ruler of all human life. Bloody wars of religion had been the aftermath of the Protestant Reformation. Amid the angry babble of discordant sectarian voices confidence in revealed religion had been lost. An idol was needed to fill the resulting vacuum. It was found in the cult of rationalism. Man was naturally good; harmony would progressively result from his autonomous actions; his reason could be trusted to find all truth and solve all problems: this in essence was the rationalistic belief of the Enlightenment.

Its complacency was shaken, however, by many untoward forces and events. Leibniz had declared this world "the best of all possible worlds," but the Lisbon earthquake, destroying a hundred thousand in a single natural catastrophe, raised a reaction of cosmic pessimism. Mandeville had maintained that private vices produced public benefits, but the immorality of the eighteenth century proved too chaotic for many good pagans. Kant the rationalist had said, "Venture to use your reason," but there was also a persistent attempt on the part of classical humanism and emotional romanticism to undermine this excessive trust in man's reason.

Indeed, Kant himself was converted by a study of Rousseau to a nonrational romanticism that sought to base religion on the sentiments of individual experience. Since reality was greater than speculative knowledge, said Kant, reason was a useless instrument in the search for truth. Thus did the sophist of Königsberg become the poisonous tap-root of modern philosophical subjectivism. He confessed in his later days: "God is not a being outside me, but merely a thought in me."[66] God had become merely his own inner idea, the *ens rationis* of his thought process, a subjective notion with no necessary transcendence of reality. Anthropocentrism could not go much further. For the next two centuries the Kantian virus infected all philosophy.

Not until Hegel came on the scene was a slightly more valid synthesis of rationalism and romanticism effected. Here was a romantic who could put emotion into logic. But he was not subjective enough for Kierkegaard, who found Hegel's continuing emphasis on the supremacy of reason intolerable. And with Kierkegaard the anti-intellectualism of the modern world begins in earnest. He falsely assumed, in his reaction to Hegel, that the speculative life of the intellect was completely cut off from reality. His contempt for the social and historical resulted in a morbid subjectivism reminiscent of Luther's early scrupulosity. His chief twentieth-century reincarnation is Karl Barth of Zurich, whose chronic pessimism springs from Luther's false teaching of the intrinsic corruption of human nature, the total depravity of man.

Add to these the irrationality of three modern philosophers—Nietzsche, Bergson, and James, who set about dethroning reason in favor of blind will to power, creative intuition, and pragmatic immediacy—stir them all together, and a witch's brew of vast potency is produced. Man's ability to control his animalistic urges is lowered with the enfeebling of his rational faculty, as also is his acuteness in pursuit of the truth and his very ability to think. Emotion takes charge; instincts run rampant; personal and social chaos result.

Nor have the newest philosophers of mathematical physics anything better to offer. Whitehead describes a God who is "Ultimate Irrationality,"[67] while Eddington and Jeans float off quite unscientifically into an illusory realm of anti-intellectual mysticism. Thus do the space-time thinkers end up with nothing but private emotional experience as their basis of belief. Fulton Sheen in his magnificent study *Philosophy of Religion* passes this judgment on anti-intellectual mysticism:

> Once void of its intellectual content, it can never *define* what it perceives, and definition is of the essence of knowledge; it can never *communicate* what it feels, for an emotional state is incommunicable. Finally, it cannot defend its truth, or distinguish it from the false, because it has repudiated the intellect which is the faculty of the true. The rational element in religion must be restored, if religion is to have any content, truth, or universality.[68]

Now the claims of the Catholic Church are based upon reason and revelation, not upon emotion or personal experience. For behind our human reason stands Divine Reason, behind our logic the eternal Logos; and this is why our rational conclusions may be followed as a reliable guide, because they truly reflect the mind of God.

That is not to say that all conversions must be by reason alone: there are many roads to faith, and grace always plays the chief part. But purely emotional religion is as unstable as human feelings, which fluctuate and change unpredictably. Where the wisdom of experience has been stored up in the subconscious, intuition may at times give reliable practical guidance. But to base a revealed religion on such subjective uncertainty is a self-evident contradiction of terms.

God is no respecter of persons: he is not a God of individual bias and subsequent social anarchy, but a God of objective truth, as this has been revealed by his Plenipotentiary Son, Jesus Christ. The seeker of truth, then, must look not to his "funny internal feelings,"[69] but to the authorized bearer of never-changing revelation and absolute law. The heat of devotional passion is a valuable adjunct of clear belief, but it is not necessary, or even possible, for all.

What hurtful heresies have been born from excessive religious emotionalism can be seen in the history of "enthusiasm." Any fanatic and fantastic foolishness can be justified by the supposed direct revelation of a supernatural "feeling." In the late second century Montanus falls into delirious inspiration and raves ecstatically: "I am the Father, the Word and the Paraclete," while Maximilla, well-born and wealthy high prophetess of his hysterical cult, declares by divine utterance: "I am the word, and spirit, and power."[70] James Nayler, harkening to the inner light of his Christ-self and thereby rejecting tradition, Scripture, and reason, is addressed by his Quaker devotees as "the fairest of ten thousand and only-begotten Son of God," shortly before they lead him upon a horse into Bristol, crying *Holy, Holy* and *Hosanna* and casting "their cloaks in the mire before him."[71] From Adam and Eve to Father Divine and his angels, *You shall be as gods* has been the root temptation. Ronald Knox in his definitive study *Enthusiasm* says this: "History abounds with warnings that the mystic who follows his own 'guidance' without any 'check' from outside may easily mistake the stirrings of his own unconscious self, even the baser of them, for inspirations from on high."[72]

Without the balancing checks of reason and authority man's own experience easily leads him astray. The blind act of faith replaces thought process, and intellect is held in distrust by those who have never learned to use the mental powers their Creator gave them. It is true that active passion must move along the path designated by the will's decision, if thought is not to be barren and fruitless. But in the stable soul, as in the stable society, reason takes precedence over feeling in order to channel it into creative, constructive deeds. Once reason has passed on the credibility of a truth, the will must decide upon accepting it and putting it into action. The mere rational possession of truth, though it is the first step, is never sufficient unto itself. "Why do you call me 'Lord, Lord,' and not do what I tell you?" "If you love me, you will keep my commandments" (Luke 6:46, John 14:15).

The Apostles' Creed, for example, is a basic summary of New Testament teaching which has always been accepted by nine-tenths of the world's professed Christians. For the beginner this creed is especially valuable as evidence of what the martyrs, saints, and suffering servants of Christ have always held in all times and places. After all, who is modern man with his provincial modern mind and individual bias of perspective, to oppose radically the testimony of this great cloud of faithful witnesses? The humble soul will accept these truths as a working hypothesis. As he grows into Christ, and into even greater fullness of truth, he will find each of these teachings to be more and more full of meaning and value for his own immediate life. And this is the point: the mere facts of the creed are like dehydrated foods which need the water of life put back into them.

Once we have found the truth with our minds, then all the passionate resolution of which we are capable should flow into action. But first we must consider the credentials of Christ and of the many churches claiming to be his. We must consider them with cold logic and the careful weighing of all the evidence. A very great tragedy of our times is that the irrationality of mass thought, prefigured by the irrationality of so many nineteenth-century Protestant and pagan philosophers, prevents spiritually sensitive souls from the judicious use of their rational faculty.

They might thereby be led to a teaching authority able to give them the one truth which alone can set them free.

C. C. Martindale summarizes this modern revolt against reason and authority:

> Luther applied the match of his rhetoric to various trains of powder, and political, social, and moral explosions occurred. His turbid genius created nothing new: his was in reality revolt against authority as such—first against the agents of the pope, then against papacy, then against the council to which he looked for help: against antiquity, against Scripture itself when it clashed with his impressionism. Despite the effort of Calvin's French logic to freeze into shape the tumultuous streams, subjectivism triumphed, and it was not so much this or that intellectual position that was stormed, as the intellect itself that was dislodged: not Rome that was defeated, so much as authority denied. Hence indubitable religious chaos. . . .[73]

4

Christ as God

The central teaching of Christianity, which all down the ages has been accepted and honored by the mainstream of Christ's followers, this normative teaching is, for many modern minds, a hard saying, an offense and a scandal. And yet this teaching is the cornerstone upon which the whole building rests. Take away this one revealed truth, and Christianity falls like a house of cards, and with it the strength of Western civilization, which is founded upon Christian truth.

The central teaching of the Christian faith is this: that the man Jesus of Nazareth, who worked as a carpenter, who ate and slept and prayed and preached and actually died on a cross like a condemned criminal, was, and is, and ever shall be, Almighty God himself.

This fact he kept hidden from his disciples for a time, because they were not ready to receive it. Had he told them right off, Jews that they were, they would have collapsed in fear before the staggering discovery of his majesty. He had first to show them by example that his very being and his every act was love. Then at last he was ready to evoke their full confession of faith, which came, however, from above as a gift from God.

Those first disciples had to learn gradually, and the full gift of faith has ever come from God; but it is difficult to see how anyone today can give himself to a study of the Scriptures, careful and open-eyed, without coming to the realization that Jesus of Nazareth *claimed* to be God in the flesh and that the early Church worshipped and adored him as such.

The earliest writings in the New Testament are by St. Paul.

Time and again the Apostle to the Gentiles tells us, unequivocally and quite plainly, that Jesus Christ is God. "Jesus, though he was in the form of God, did not count equality with God a thing to be grasped"—in other words, he did not disdain to become a man—"but emptied himself, taking the form of a servant, being born in the likeness of men" (Phil. 2:5–7).

This central teaching is so important to Paul that he warns the Christians at Colossae against those who would corrupt their faith and insinuate false doubts into their minds. "See to it that no one makes a prey of you by philosophy and empty deceit, according to human tradition, according to the elemental spirits of the universe, and not according to Christ. For in him the whole fulness of deity dwells bodily" (Col. 2:8–9).

"Obviously," the skeptical modern will say, "that Pharisee Paul corrupted the Christian religion by making Jesus into God."

Consider, then, what those claimed for the Master who traveled with him and shared his daily round, when he lived the life of a man on this whirling ball called earth. St. John, the disciple who was closer to the Master's heart than any other, describes him as being the Word of God, the Word with which God the Father utters himself. In the first chapter of his gospel John tells us that this Word always existed with the Father, that there was never a time when the Word was not. Then the Second Person of the Trinity "became flesh and dwelt among us, full of grace and truth" (John 1:14). Since "the Word was with God, and the Word was God" (John 1:1), "all may honor the Son, even as they honor the Father" (John 5:23).

John tells us about the skeptical Thomas at the end of his gospel, or good news, story. It seems that Thomas would not believe that Jesus was still alive, though he had previously assured his followers: "I lay down my life, that I might take it again. . . . I have power to lay it down, and I have power to take it again" (John 10:17–18). "So the other disciples told him, 'We have seen the Lord.' But he said to them, 'Unless I see in his hands the print of the nails, and place my finger in the mark of the nails, and place my hand in his side, I will not believe.' Eight days later, his disciples were again in the house, and Thomas was with them. The doors were shut, but Jesus came and stood among them, and said, 'Peace be with you.' Then he said to Thomas, 'Put your finger here, and see my hands; and put out your hand, and place it in my side; do not be faithless, but believing.' Thomas answered him, 'My Lord and my God!' Jesus said to him, 'Have you believed because you have seen me? Blessed are those who have not seen and yet believe' " (John 20:25–29).

Here the risen Jesus, during one of his physical reappearances, commends a man who calls him God to his face and offers him adoration. How many times in the gospels it says of his disciples that they worshipped him! This "worshipping" may not have included "adoration," but it certainly paid him high honor. "The eleven disciples . . . when they saw him . . . worshiped him" (Matt. 28:16–17). "A ruler came in and knelt before him" (Matt. 9:18). "A leper came to him and knelt before him" (Matt. 8:2).

Of course, those who were not so close to our Lord rarely paid him this honor. They were much more apt to hate him when they got to know him, as the world hates all those who refuse to follow its erroneous way. This is why the man from Nazareth made so many enemies. Being God, he refused to agree with the world he had made when that world was wrong. He insisted on changing things that needed to be changed. He did offer comfort to the troubled and the disturbed, but he also disturbed and troubled the comfortable. He came to a people satisfied with their evil ways, and he said to them: "Unless one is born anew, he cannot see the kingdom of God" (John 3:3). "Enter by the narrow gate; for the gate is wide and the way is easy, that leads to destruction, and those who enter by it are many. For the gate is narrow and the way is hard, that leads to life, and those who find it are few" (Matt. 7:13–14). This is why the man from Nazareth was always making enemies: no one cares to hear that sort of message, whether it be true or not. This is one of the chief reasons why men sent him to the cross. He rejected the false beliefs of a sick society, claiming that he himself was truth in the form of a man. "I am the way, and the truth, and the life," he said. "No one comes to the Father, but by me" (John 14:6).

Even the Pharisees admitted the fact that Jesus *claimed* to be God, but they attributed his miracles to the Devil and refused to accept his claims. They believed, as did all good Jews, that only God could forgive sins, because only God could see into a man's heart, and only he had the right to erase an infinite offense against his own Majesty. And yet, here was this presumptuous rabbi from Nazareth, who went about telling people their sins were forgiven and healing their infirmities by his miraculous power. How amazing were those mighty works of his! "The works which the Father has granted me to accomplish," he said, "these very works which I am doing, bear me witness that the Father has sent me" (John 5:36).

After the blind man had been healed by the sheep market pool at Bethsaida, after his sins had been forgiven and his sight restored, he stumbled on his way with new eyes and told the Jews that it was Jesus who had wrought this prodigy of healing in his body. "This was why the Jews sought all the more to kill him, because he not only broke the sabbath but also called God his Father, making himself equal with God" (John 5:18). Here we have this pretentious claim again, that he is equal to God, because he is the Son of God.

"Now there you've hit it," the skeptical modern will say. "Jesus said he was the Son of God. He wasn't God: he was the Son of God."

And yet he claimed "that God was his Father, making himself equal with God." When the faithful Christian says the words "God is my Father," he does not say them in a way that makes him equal with God. For after all, that would be blasphemy, and besides, it is quite evident that he is not all-knowing and all-powerful.

But that is exactly what Jesus did. He never claimed to be *a* son of God: he claimed to be *the* Son of God, the one and only Son of God, of the same nature and power as his heavenly Father, as we created beings are not and never shall be. Jesus claimed to be *the Son* from all eternity; he said there never was a time when he did not exist: "Before Abraham was, I am" (John 8:58). He represented himself constantly as being sent down to this earth on a special mission from heaven in order to save men from their sins and to conquer the powers of spiritual darkness. He called himself the light of the world. He invited all men to come to him that they might find rest and peace. He claimed the power to forgive sin and raise the dead. He promised the joys of heaven to any and all who believed in him and his authorized messengers.

Even on the day of his deepest disgrace, Jesus proclaimed himself to be the Source of truth, the Ruler and Judge of mankind. Caiaphas, the high priest, said to his prisoner: " 'I adjure you by the living God, tell us if you are the Christ, the Son of God.' Jesus said to him, 'You have said so. But I tell you, hereafter you will see the Son of man seated at the right hand of Power, and coming on the clouds of heaven' " (Matt. 26:63–64). Here the Messiah, who had called himself both the Son of man and the Son of God, because he was both perfect Man and perfect God, tells once again of the Last Judgment of souls, himself being the Supreme Judge. For as he often claimed, God the Father had given all judgment to God the Son.

He also told his disciples this: "All authority in heaven and on earth has been given to me" (Matt. 28:18). This all-powerful Sovereign of Creation, by whom, according to Scripture, the worlds were made (Col. 1:16), was nevertheless capable of the most amazing, the most astounding, humility. Under the sign of weakness and in the form of a helpless newborn infant, he entered his own world. Thus did he make himself small so that men could understand God in their own terms.

> All praise to Thee, Eternal Lord,
> Clothed in a garb of flesh and blood;
> Choosing a manger for Thy throne,
> While worlds on worlds are Thine alone.

Once did the skies before Thee bow;
A Virgin's arms contain Thee now:
Angels who did in Thee rejoice
Now listen for Thine infant voice.[74]

Having become a little child, he continued to humble himself throughout his sojourn among men by living a life of utter obedience to his heavenly Father, even to the extreme of going to his death as a common criminal. Yet all during his lowly walk on this earth, he longed for the day when his prayer would be answered: "And now, Father, glorify thou me in thy own presence with the glory which I had with thee before the world was made" (John 17:5).

As a man upon earth, Christ Jesus worshipped his Father in heaven. There was nothing to stop this Man from worshipping God the Father. In meekness he referred everything to his Father and said that he was only doing his Father's will and works. Thus did he set for all his followers an example of obedience. Yet at the same time he assured them with the voice of authority: "He who has seen me has seen the Father" (John 14:9).

Jesus Christ claimed to be God in the flesh. His coming was accurately foretold among the Jews by prophetic voices from many times and places. His character was sinless and perfectly God-centered in every thought, word, and deed. His message contained the highest and holiest precepts, motivations, and aids of grace the world has ever known. Granted that he was neither an impostor nor a lunatic, his claim to be God, upheld by demonstrated foreknowledge of the future, confirmed by many superhuman miracles, and sealed by resurrection from the dead, would seem to be irrefutable.

It is no wonder that, from the very first, Christ himself was the object of worship, prayer, and praise; so much so that the early Christians were referred to by the Roman administrator Pliny in A.D. 112 as people "who sang hymns to Christ as God."

The Christian religion stands or falls by this cornerstone teaching. Where the truth about our Divine Lord's nature has been diluted and emasculated until he is considered to be little more than a mere man like others, there Christianity grows weak and eventually dies out. Such apostasy of belief is not unknown among the sects; whereas the Roman Church has never deserted this sound and central truth. For twenty centuries she has offered up to her Founder the honor and glory which rightfully are his.

And now in what remains of this book, I shall concern myself chiefly with those doctrines and practices of the Catholic Church which present most difficulty to Protestants, upon which I had especially to clear my own mind.

5

Peter's Primacy

Writes Oscar Cullmann, Professor in Basel and Paris, foremost Lutheran scholar and one of Protestantism's most distinguished historians:

> I hold that in addition to the ecumenical achievements of recent decades it is precisely the simple discussion between Catholic and Protestant theologians that is one of the encouraging events in the church history of our time . . . A resumption of the discussion concerning the primacy of Rome is also advisable because the arguments are no longer the same as they were in the sixteenth and seventeenth centuries.[75]

In his book *Peter* Cullmann insists that our most reliable modern scholarship leads to the conclusion that Peter himself was indeed the Rock on which Christ founded his Church, that he exercised primacy among the apostles until he left Jerusalem for his missionary work, which eventually led him to Rome, where he died a martyr.

The chief question, however, he faces but half-heartedly: Would our Lord have provided such a rocklike leader for a short time only, having guaranteed that the powers of death would *never* prevail against his Church? Dr. Cullmann comes up to this jump at a full gallop and then balks.

> It is arguing in a circle . . . to assert that, since on the one hand the promise of Jesus to Peter exists, and on the other hand the fact exists that Rome exercised a primacy from a relatively early date, we therefore must conclude that this primacy rests on that promise. . . . In the life of Peter there is no starting-point for a chain of succession to the leadership of the Church at large.[76]

Peter's Roman martyrdom he fully accepts, after examining minutely all the evidence available. "Were we to demand for all facts of ancient history a greater degree of probability, we should have to strike from our history books a large proportion of their contents."[77] The grave of Peter, he claims, cannot be identified. But the excavations at the Vatican, which have been progressing carefully since 1939, have brought many competent scholars to a firm belief that here indeed, protected by the "red wall" are the trophies and the relics of the chief apostle. Only a few pieces of bone remain, but "these human remains cannot be considered but the remains of St. Peter. No one else has ever been buried here."[78]

At any rate, Peter was primate in Jerusalem and died in Rome as a martyr under Nero.

When did his primacy begin? St. John in his gospel says that at the very first moment in which Jesus beheld Peter, he said: " 'So you are Simon the son of John? You shall be called Cephas' (which means Peter)" (John 1:42). Only later did our Lord explain the full meaning of this noun-word *Kepha*, which at that time was not yet in use as a proper name.

But it very early became evident that Peter was to stand in the foreground of the inner circle of followers. As spokesman he was to represent the other disciples, to ask and to answer for them. Whenever the disciples are referred to, Peter is always listed first. "The names of the twelve apostles are these: first, Simon, who is called Peter . . ." (Matt. 10:2). He is often singled out for special emphasis, as where the angel says: "But go, tell his disciples and Peter that he is going before you to Galilee" (Mark 16:7). Peter, furthermore, acts as spokesman for the other disciples, saying: "Lord, are you telling this parable for us or for all?" (Luke 12:41), and "Lo, we have left everything and followed you. What then shall we have?" (Matt. 19:27).

Our Lord singles him out time after time. Peter is taken to the mount of transfiguration and the garden of Gethsemane, where he bears rebuke for the other disciples: "Could you not watch with me one hour?" (Matt. 26:40). He is enabled by his Master to walk on the water, and he is the first to confess that Jesus is the Christ, the Son of the living God.

The Carpenter of Nazareth well knew how important it was to build his house upon a rock: "Every one then who hears these words of mine and does them will be like a wise man who built his house upon the rock; and the rain fell, and the winds blew and beat upon that house, but it did not fall, because it had been founded on the rock" (Matt. 7:24–25).

This is why Jesus made Peter the Church's pivotal authority. "You are Peter, and on this rock I will build my church" (Matt. 16:18). After the Resurrection, Peter is singled out to receive the charge: "Feed my sheep" (John 21:15–17).

No strength of his own merited these honors. Impulsive, changeable, enthusiastic, full of a fiery but unstable zeal—in his own weakness Peter was anything but a Rock. His triple denial shows that quite clearly. Therefore, his pre-eminence must have resulted from the purpose of his Master, rather than from any strength of his own.

A great undergirding of Peter's character occurs after the Resurrection appearances and the triple affirmation of John 21. He occupies the presiding chair of leadership at Jerusalem, exercises discipline over Ananias and Sapphira, initiates the mission to the Gentiles, considers how best to protect Jewish Christians from the persecution of the zealots, mediates between Judaizers and Hellenists,[79] and makes far-reaching policy decisions for the whole Church. The faith of the people in his miraculous powers was boundless. "So that they even carried out the sick into the streets, and laid them on beds and pallets, that as Peter came by at least his shadow might fall on some of them" (Acts 5:15).

The shadow of Peter has been cast by the Sun of Righteousness down the long vistas of two millenniums of Western Church history. "When he saw the crowds, he had compassion for them, because they were harassed and helpless, like sheep without a shepherd" (Matt. 9:36). Our Lord knew how this need for guidance was ageless and continuing. He therefore provided that after his Ascension there should be a visible Chief Shepherd. "I am the good shepherd," he had said; "I know my own and my own know me . . . I lay down my life for the sheep. . . . So there shall be one flock, one shepherd" (John 10:14–16) Then to Peter before his departure: "Feed my sheep" (John 21:15–17). Thus was the rod and staff transferred to Peter for the stability and unity of the early Church.

St. Augustine makes this observation from the study of history: "The enemies of the Church themselves die and disappear, but the Church itself lives on, and preaches the power of God to every succeeding generation." Christ told Peter that the powers of death would never conquer his Church, and he did not limit that Church's duration. Are we, then, to assume that the stable leadership and unity which he provided in Peter were to end when Peter left Jerusalem for his missionary work? Were these necessities of survival promised for one generation only— or for all times, even unto the end of the world? Does the later Church of the Middle Ages and modern times have less need of a head than the early Church of the apostles, who had walked and talked with Christ in the flesh? When he gave to his chief follower the power of the keys, of binding and loosing, did Jesus have in mind, along with Peter, his successors?

Our Lord prayed for the unity of those who should follow the original apostles, that the world might believe their message. "I do not pray for these only, but also for those who believe in me through their word" (John 17:20). He who had come down from above to reveal God's truth would surely have made provision for its safe transmission. There is no record of his ever commanding his apostles to write a book, and he never wrote one himself while he lived here on earth. But he did commission a teaching society and promised them his abiding presence for all generations. He warned them against departing from his original message and plan, against omitting even the slightest truth he had given them: they must teach men to observe "all that I have commanded you" (Matt. 28:20).

The society he had gathered and founded in the Twelve must agree among themselves, if they were to remain one, and they were sent forth to teach, as Christ had done, with authority. "As the Father has sent me, even so I send you" (John 20:21). "He who hears you hears me" (Luke 10:16). "Go into all the world and preach the gospel to the whole creation. He who believes and is baptized will be saved; but he who does not believe will be condemned" (Mark 16:15–16). It would seem reasonable that God would command belief under pain of condemnation only if he intended to make provision for the pure and undefiled transmission of his divine word. He desires that all men should "come to the knowledge of the truth" (1 Tim. 2:4), and he commands his society to teach them this truth, praying that they may be undivided, since "Every kingdom divided against itself is laid waste, and no city or house divided against itself will stand" (Matt. 12:25).

Our Lord provided for this unified authority in the first generation through Peter, who was called as chief shepherd of the flock, to feed and strengthen the sheep, and to whom Christ gave the keys, an accepted symbol and sign of governing authority. The historical fact is that successors of Peter continued to exercise his functions without the objection of the churches. They probably reasoned that if the Founder of their society bequeathed them group unity through establishing a chief leader, then who were they to alter the pattern he had initiated? It is certainly not "arguing in a circle" to say the early Church Fathers accepted the bishops of Rome as the rightful successors of Peter. They did not sink into the anarchy of leaderless sectarianism but clung to that pivotal authority which they believed God himself had established and continued to uphold. They desired to imitate the apostolic age in having only one faith, "one flock, one shepherd" (John 10:16). The pre-eminence of the Roman Church and her bishops continued after Peter's death, while the papacy itself gradually developed and matured with time, as must any live and growing social organism.

Acorns develop into oaks, caterpillars change into butterflies, and babies grow eventually into rational adults. Likewise the Roman Church has matured and unfolded with time. Its doctrinal developments are not additions to the original deposit of faith but only the further unwrapping of that glorious gift. As Newman said in his great *Essay on the Development of Christian Doctrine:* "Time is necessary for the full comprehension and perfection of great ideas." Their development in time is not corruption,[80] as Protestants erroneously maintain, but the surest evidence of life and energy. It is lack of growth and change which signifies the approach of death.

In the early centuries the papacy may have been a child exercising fewer prerogatives than it now exercises, but it was nevertheless the same entity—Simon Peter and his successors in the pre-eminent Roman bishopric. The testimony of the early Fathers on their continuing allegiance to this Roman Church and its leader is available for all to examine.

Within a generation of Peter's martyrdom, his third successor, Clement I, writes to the distant Corinthians, claiming obedience from them to "what we, prompted by the Holy Spirit, have written" (1 Clement 63:2), and warning them that if there be any "who fail to obey what God has told them *through us,* they must realize that they will enmesh themselves in sin and in no insignificant danger" (1 Clement 59:1).[81]

St. Ignatius of Antioch, half a generation later, well knew the importance of the Church's being one. "Make unity your concern —there is nothing better than that" (Letter to Polycarp 1:25).[82] "Where the bishop is present, there let the congregation gather, just as where Jesus Christ is, there is the Catholic Church. It is a fine thing to acknowledge God and the bishop. He who pays the bishop honor has been honored by God. But he who acts without the bishop's knowledge is in the devil's service" (Letter to Smyrnaeans 8:2; 9:1).[83]

St. Irenaeus, who sat at the feet of Polycarp in Smyrna, says of the Roman Church: "With this Church, on account of its pre-eminent authority, it is necessary that every Church should be in concord." He affirms that "the apostolic tradition is preserved in it," and that the faith of Peter and Paul, who established it, "comes down to us through the successions of bishops" (*Adversus Haereses*).

In the third century St. Cyprian, bishop of Carthage, says of the Roman Church: "It is the root and mother of the Catholic Church, the chair of Peter, and the principal Church whence sacerdotal unity has its source." Leo XIII, in his lucid Encyclical Letter on the unity of the Church, *Sates Cognitum*, comments as follows:

> He calls it *the chair of Peter* because it is occupied by the successor of Peter; he calls it the *principal Church* on account of the primacy conferred on Peter himself and his legitimate successors; and *the source of unity*, because the Roman Church is the efficient cause of unity in the Christian commonwealth.[84]

The greatest scholar among the Fathers, Jerome, writes thus: "My words are spoken to the successor of the Fisherman. . . . I communicate with none save your Blessedness, that is with the chair of Peter. For this I know is the rock on which the Church is built. . . . I acknowledge everyone who is united with the See of Peter."[85]

Augustine of Hippo, beloved authority of so many Protestants, also witnesses to his belief that "the primacy of the apostolic chair always existed in the Roman Church."[86]

Such is the testimony of the Fathers to the continuing primacy of the Roman bishops. The General Councils corroborate this evidence. From Ephesus in 431 come these words: "There is no doubt that the holy and most blessed Peter, Prince and Chief of the apostles, received the keys of the kingdom, and that until the present time he always lives and judges his successors." From Chalcedon in 451 we hear that "Peter has spoken through Leo." It is difficult to see how Protestants who assert the authority of these early General Councils can, at the same time, reject their evident adherence to the doctrine of papal primacy.

If a choice must be made between (1) this clear witness of Fathers and Councils, and (2) the discordant, contradictory testimonies of men who agree chiefly in refusing submission to the pope—what reasonable man, once he clearly sees the facts, can long hesitate? Can an interpretation of Scripture possibly be correct which portrays the changeless Holy Spirit of Truth as working through division and disagreement, saying "yes" to one sect and "no" to another on the same questions? Can the Holy Spirit teach such contradictions as these: that Jesus Christ is both God and no more than a mere man; that he is corporeally present in Holy Communion and that he is only spiritually present; that bishops and sacraments are scriptural and neither are needed; that man is a sinner and naturally good; that the ordained are to pronounce absolution and God uses no secondary mediators in confession; that apostolic succession is necessary and useless; that marriage is indissoluble and divorce permitted; that Christ enjoined fasting and did not; that good works are meritorious and of no avail; that children may be baptized and adults only; that man has been given free will and is absolutely predestined; that hell is terrible and does not exist; and so forth *ad infinitum?* Is the Holy Spirit of Jesus Christ the author of this confusion confounded? Protestantism, supposedly led by this Holy Spirit, teaches all these things—and agrees only in refusing submission to that one authority which Christ established for the purpose of leading Christians into his own certainty.

Our Lord spoke with authority and revealed definite teachings. He expected his Church to do likewise. He did not commission his ambassadors to hem and haw with "maybe," "perhaps," "to the best of my knowledge," and "it seems to me." He expected them to affirm divine revelation, which cannot contradict itself. "You will know the truth," he said, "and the truth will make you free" (John 8:32)—free from the destructive dogmatisms of modernity, free from the autonomous attempts to fabricate one's own faith and morality, free of the inner fears and social anarchies that result from ultimate uncertainty.

The Catholic Church is the only society that can rightfully claim to speak in the manner of the Master. It does so by virtue of the chair of Peter and through his successors. It has spoken with this sure authority on faith and morals since A.D. 33.

The papacy is the one institutional office in our world today that has endured for the past two thousand years. There have been quite a few immoral popes and several periods of clerical corruption, but the successors of St. Peter teach on. Customs change, ideas vary, purposes proliferate, loyalties die, people come and go, movements wax and wane, nations rise and fall, dictators disappear, and empires crumble—but the papacy endures. Who can account for this most amazing fact of the ages without referring to the purpose and power of God? Surely it is his hand alone which upholds the successors of Peter, to whom Our Divine Lord said: "You are Peter, and on this rock I will build my church, and the powers of death shall not prevail against it" (Matt. 16:18).

6

Impregnable Rock

The last of the Victorians, William Inge, the contrary, "gloomy dean" of St. Paul's Cathedral in London, based his beliefs too much upon the quicksands of mystic subjectivism. The private intuition of inner experience was his chief authority. In *Christian Mysticism*, before the nineteenth century had ended, he wrote:

> We cannot shut our eyes to the fact that both the old seats of authority, the infallible Church and the infallible book, are fiercely assailed, and that our faith needs reinforcements. These can only come from the depths of the religious consciousness itself; and if summoned from thence, they will not be found wanting. The "impregnable rock" is neither an institution nor a book, but a life of experience.[87]

The proliferation of contradictory sects and the social chaos of our modern world have been the result of such autonomous subjectivism. Where each man becomes his own pope through a following of inner lights, anarchy reigns supreme among men. As in the story of the tower of Babel, everyone speaks, but no one understands his neighbor, nor his God.

Some authority there must be to bring order out of individualism's anarchy. The soul itself ever searches for sure footing, and where it does not find this in objective truth and revealed moral law, it sinks into the quicksands of uncertainty. But man was not made to be "tossed to and fro and carried about with every wind of doctrine" (Eph. 4:14); he was not meant to "listen to anybody and . . . never arrive at a knowledge of the truth" (2 Tim. 3:7).

Jesus Christ came into the world to "bear witness to the truth" (John 18:37). He taught definite doctrines. He sent his ambassadors forth to disseminate "*all* that I have commanded" (Matt. 28:20, emphasis added). He said that salvation depended upon believing these revealed facts (Mark 16:16). God wills all men to be saved (1 Tim. 2:4); he cannot mean them to cling to falsehood and error.

In order to accept God's truth men must first know in an absolutely certain way what it is.

"Anything short of complete certainty is uncertainty."[88] The bearer of dogma must be able to prove beyond a shadow of a doubt that his interpretation is the correct one. If a man will be damned and lose God forever by not believing (Mark 16:16), he will want to be double-check sure that what he accepts is really God's truth and not just one more human opinion. He will think it foolhardy in the extreme to accept any teaching as coming from the mouth of God unless he is perfectly certain that the Omniscient really did say it in exactly that way. For if God, who cannot deceive, stands behind a truth and expresses it to men through a trustworthy channel, then, and then alone, can men be sure of being on the right road home. Probabilities are not enough for "assured understanding" (Col. 2:2). Certainty based upon God-given authority is required.

Sensing this need for an infallible authority, the Protestant Reformers of the sixteenth century turned to the Bible. They said, as the Roman Church had always said, that Holy Scripture was an inspired, inerrant word. It was the vehicle for a divine message, and its ultimate author was God.

Jesus Christ himself asserted its absolute authority (Matt. 5:18; Luke 24:44; John 10:35), and he explained its true meaning to his disciples (Luke 24:27, 45). But he did not found his religion upon a book. He never wrote a word and never commanded his inner circle to write. The apostles never distributed a single copy of the Bible, but they preached and taught everywhere with the authority of those who had been sent. Their Lord had not said, "If a man will not read the scriptures, let him be to you as a Gentile and a tax collector," but, "if he refuses to listen even to the church" (Matt. 18:17).

The Reformation, however, taught that the chief channel of revelation and the only rule of faith was the Bible, as it was interpreted by the private judgment of each separate reader. Luther called his own interpretations authoritative, as did Calvin, but neither of them made their viewpoints stick very long. After all, the clergy as a class with authority to teach was implicitly abolished by the doctrine of the priesthood of all believers. Henceforth, the Holy Ghost was expected to guide even the most illinformed illiterate into correct understanding. This false expectation has brought about countless contradictory interpretations within Protestantism of almost every vital point in Scripture. Peter the Rock well knew how many things in the Bible were "hard to understand" by the "ignorant and unstable" (2 Pet. 3:16). He therefore warned the Church of the invalidity and unwisdom of "one's own interpretation" (2 Pet. 1:20).

Holy Scripture without a living interpreter is no practical authority at all, but merely a dead letter. Protestants do not even know that Scripture is the reliable word of God except by the authority of the Catholic Church, which wrote, collected, and endorsed the books of the New Testament. Certainty on what was to be included in the canon of Scripture was not reached until several centuries after our Lord's death. Where did those early saints and martyrs learn God's truth? From the teaching Church. Copies of the Bible were not readily available until the invention of papermaking and printing. Did our Lord leave the first millennium and a half of Christians without a book whose authority was the only means of salvation? He did not. He directed their attention to the teaching Church, which was the mother of the New Testament, and out of whose ongoing life it was born.

The Church, then, existed prior to the New Testament, and she is the rightful custodian of it. Jesus Christ did not build his Church on the sands of private interpretation. He followed the advice he had given others to build upon a rock (Matt. 7:24). He built upon Peter, to whom he gave the power of binding and loosing (Matt. 16:19). In the rabbinical usage of his day these terms meant to make laws that bind and to dispense from or rewrite them. "Whatever you bind on earth," he said to Peter, "shall be bound in heaven." By these words Jesus Christ promised to ratify after his Ascension the decisions of his chief shepherd on earth.

Thus quite plainly he gave divine authority to Peter, and along with it infallibility. For how could God the Son, who said, "I am the truth," countersign anything false? And yet he promised to endorse all of Peter's binding decisions. Inescapable logic leads to the conclusion that Peter would not be allowed to decide falsely, that in certain circumstances he must, in fact, be infallible. For this "unfailability" our Lord prayed: "I have prayed for you that your faith may not fail" (Luke 22:32). And his prayers are always answered.

The Catholic Church maintains this teaching in an extremely mild form. How slight the infallibility of the pope really is, according to Catholic teaching, few Protestants understand. It rarely involves any direct intervention by God, who simply watches over his instrument to prevent him, if necessary, from making a mistake in vital teaching. The pope, like any other man, must search out the truths he teaches. He has, however, whole batteries of scholars and the tradition of two thousand years to guide him. When his investigations on any controversial matter are finished, and in his capacity as Chief Teacher of the universal Church he announces his binding decision in a question of faith or morals, then by the assurance given to St. Peter and his successors, the Holy Spirit will not allow him to speak falsely, lest the whole body of believers be led astray, and the powers of death prevail against the Church, and the promise of Christ be proved invalid (Matt. 16:18).

The pope is thus protected from erroneous teaching, not when he speaks privately, nor usually when he speaks publicly, but only when, as leader of the faithful and in his official capacity, he pinpoints a truth of faith or morals, builds it irreformably into the structure of the Church, and declares that all must believe his definition upon pain of excommunication.

When disagreements arise and heretics attack the agelong Christian beliefs, such definitions are essential if purity of doctrine is to be preserved. The Holy Spirit, Catholics maintain, thus guarantees the teaching even of immoral and worldly popes, lest the faithful be left to flounder in their doubts, and the Church collapse. For it is not the man but the office which is guaranteed by God. It is not the pope who is honored by this special grace but the individual believer, who is thus protected against shipwreck of faith upon the reefs and shoals of uncertainty and falsehood. Peter's bark will give its occupants safe and sure passage. It will never sink. For the Master Mariner is with the helmsman today just as surely as he was two thousand years ago on the Sea of Galilee (Matt. 8:23–27).

If this is true, then the chief Protestant objection to the Catholic position, that it has corrupted the original gospel by man-made accretion, is obviously an illogical protest. Infallibility does not exclude the development and unfolding of tradition and implicit scriptural truth, but it does make impossible the projection of mythological illusion into the original deposit of faith. Saints have been deceived and taught falsely; individual bishops have countenanced heresy; even popes have seemed for a moment to follow the serpent's path into the wilderness of error—but no official and binding pronouncement, spoken *ex cathedra*, has ever had to be retracted or subsequently abandoned. In every decisive theological controversy of Christian history the bishops of Rome have been on the right side, and usually they have been there ahead of their contemporaries.[89] Changes of doctrinal and devotional *emphasis* have been many, but changes of truth have never occurred. The Protestant appeal to history shatters upon the solid rock of this fundamental fact.

Being a living organism like a plant or a tree, the Church has grown and flowered according to its nature. When challenged by counteraffirmations, doctrines always accepted have been defined. But nothing new has ever been added: "Definition no more makes new doctrine than does a new treatise on geometry make new mathematical truth."[90] Basic innovations have never been introduced. The heresiarchs have been the innovators, shocking and disturbing those generations to which they have made their novel appeals. Marcion, Montanus, Sabellius, Arius, Nestorius, Eutyches, Pelagius, Photius, Valdez, Wycliff, Hus, Luther, Calvin, Henry VIII—these have been the innovators, corrupters, distorters, and false prophets, attacking the unity for which he prayed whose prayers are always answered. Like gigantic waves they have, each in his turn, dashed themselves against the impregnable rock of papal infallibility, there to shatter and disintegrate in a showy but ultimately ineffectual froth of flying foam. In the end heresies always disappear.

Hilaire Belloc puts it this way:

> I submit that no matter what particular defined doctrine in the Catholic scheme you may select, you will find without exception this most notable character attaching to it, that when denial of it was made within the Christian community—as when Arius denied the consubstantiality of the Son, or as when Nestorius denied the divine motherhood of our Lady—it had the effect of a stone thrown at a pane of glass and breaking it: the startling effect of a shock; of something quite unexpected and exceedingly and unpleasantly new.[91]

But after the first fine flurry of adolescent revolt, the inescapable laws of nature work slowly but surely against the merely human novelty: rapid growth is succeeded by decay and decline, until only a few half-hearted adherents remain to protest the supposed arrogance and idolatry of Rome. Such is ever the fate of those who, refusing to "endure sound teaching," turn from God's truth unto fables of human invention (2 Tim. 4:3−4).

Jesus Christ is the same yesterday, today, and forever; and from age to age his providential instrument, the papacy, carries on as the unshakeable foundation of Christian certainty, teaching the faithful what they must accept and embody as true thought and good action if they are to please their Maker. The unity that the head thus ensures the body is a visible unity, the continuation of the Incarnation. It is of this visible Church which St. Paul speaks when he tells the Ephesian elders: "Take heed to yourselves and to all the flock, in which the Holy Spirit has made you guardians, to feed the church of the Lord which he obtained with his own blood" (Acts 20:28). It is this visible society which must remain one, so that the pagan world may see it, marvel, and believe (John 17:21). If the Church were not readily recognizable, how could a man be condemned for not believing what it taught? (Matt. 18:17; Mark 16:18). And if it were meant to be invisible, as Luther and Calvin falsely maintained, would it be compared by Christ to so many hard external realities, such as a net, a tree, a treasure, a body, a flock, a fold, a house, a bride, a kingdom? As God was Incarnate and made visible for all to see, so also his Church, like a "city set on a hill cannot be hid" (Matt. 5:14), confronts the world seeking recognition.

Yes, Jesus Christ intended to found a visible Church on earth, which was to be his Mystical Body, the extension of the Incarnation. According to St. Matthew, he spoke of it as the "kingdom of heaven." He compared this "kingdom of heaven" to a field of wheat and tares (Matt. 13:24-30) and to a net containing good and bad fish (Matt. 13:47-50). He likened it to ten virgins, five of them wise and five of them foolish (Matt. 25:1-13). Certainly he could not have meant a solely supernatural realm, for in God's other eternal world there are no evil tares, no bad fish, no foolish virgins. In using the expression "kingdom of heaven," then, our divine Lord was quite evidently referring to his Church, that visible and universal organism which he was creating. This is plain from his words to Peter: "I will give you the keys of the *kingdom of heaven*, [by which he meant his Church] and whatever you bind *on earth* shall be bound in heaven" (Matt. 16:19). The early Fathers understood him this way. St. John Chrysostom speaks for them when he assures us: "It is easier for the sun to be quenched than for the Church to be made invisible."

How monstrous it would appear for a visible body to lack a visible head! But in Peter and his successors, according to Catholic teaching, we have the visible head and audible voice of the One, Holy, Catholic, and Apostolic Church, which is the Mystical Body of our risen Lord. When the pope speaks to define and explain "the faith which was once for all delivered to the saints" (Jude 3), he is protected by God from leading this visible society into error.

The Vatican Council of 1870 stated this Catholic belief in precise terms, when the assembled bishops issued their authoritative definition.

> Adhering faithfully to the doctrine handed down from the beginning of the Christian faith, we teach and define that it is a truth revealed by God that the bishop of Rome, when he speaks ex cathedra, that is to say when he acts in his official capacity as Shepherd and Teacher of all Christians, and uses his supreme apostolic authority to decree that a piece of teaching concerning faith or morality is to be accepted by the whole Church, then, because of the divine assistance promised to him in St. Peter, he enjoys that infallibility which the divine Redeemer willed his Church to have in defining teaching about faith and morality; and therefore such definitions of the bishop of Rome are unchangeable of themselves, and not because the Church accepts them.

As St. Paul had said: "If any one is preaching to you a gospel contrary to that which you received, let him be accursed" (Gal. 1:9); so the bishops ended their pronouncements with the statement: "If anyone presume to contradict this definition of ours, which God forbid, let him be anathema."[92]

7

Freedom in Truth

Human bondage is proverbial. No one is completely free. Men are unable to jump over the moon; they cannot breathe poisonous gasses and live; they are not allowed to repeal the laws of nature. The liberty the Creator has given the creature is a liberty within laws. Men cannot break the natural or moral laws of God without in their turn being broken upon them. Neither can they reject God's accredited messengers and the binding laws of Christ's own Church without falling into error and ignorance. Those who lead men into such rebellion are the real reactionaries, reacting as they do against God's own truth and authority. Such false prophets are the real perpetuators of human bondage. For man is never truly free except where he voluntarily obeys the will of God.

There is great freedom of thought within the unity of Catholicism. Benedictines, Franciscans, Dominicans, Jesuits—these orders are in vital and fruitful competition. Not that they have been given license to believe what is false or teach what has been declared heretical. They all teach, for example, and that man has been given free will by God, that in order to keep this freedom the teachings of the Church must be followed. In areas where the fullness of truth has not been defined they vie in scholarship and creativity. In Catholic universities "academic freedom" should not be a cloak for chaos, but a stimulus to ordered investigation along worthwhile channels. Magisterial authority protects the Catholic scholar, as Newman remarks in his *Apologia*. "Its object is, and its effect also, not to enfeeble the freedom or vigor of human thought, but to resist and control its extravagances." Within this healthy limitation the dedicated Catholic mind is open not only to search after the truth, but to embrace it at all costs. The exercise of private judgment in legitimate areas of uncertainty is commended and encouraged by the Roman Church. As Arnold Lunn explains it:

> It is only when the Catholic has established by reason the existence of an infallible Church that he surrenders his private judgment to the judgment of the Church, on those points, and on those points only, on which the Church speaks with the voice of God. In all other questions private judgment still remains supreme.[93]

As for political freedom, direct papal control does not intrude itself beyond the Papal State into the outer temporal world: this is not its rightful sphere. Certainly American Catholics owe no civil allegiance to Rome, and they recognize no right or power by which the pope might interfere with the operation of the laws of the land or the contents of the Constitution.

In the late eleventh century Hildebrand, who as Pope Gregory VII proved himself to be a monk-reformer of noble character and clear purpose, may have misconstrued his office as having a theocratic obligation to depose unworthy rulers and absolve their subjects from fealty.[94] That kind of subordination of the State to the Church is not recognized by St. Paul, who declares that political rulers have their authority directly from God by reason of their responsibility for the temporal common good (Rom. 13:1–6). Christ's kingdom is not of this world primarily, and Peter's successors were never meant to have such vast temporal powers. On the contrary, they have been told by their Master to "render to Caesar the things that are Caesar's" (Mark 12:17).

In the inner world of man's soul the "I" should exercise an absolute rulership in truth, refusing equal rights to wayward impulse and evil thought. But in the outer world of man's society such political totalitarianism is disastrous, making an idol of the state and a slave of the individual. Throughout history the confusion of these two worlds, operating upon diametrically opposed systems of organization, has brought in its wake unhappy results. Projecting their "I" into the outer world, "tyrants have tried persistently to capture all of humanity, and all of humanity at times has demonstrated a tendency to submit itself to dictatorship."[95] This is most apt to happen in eras of unbelief, because then the inner chaos of uncertainty produces outer disorders and leads men to seek social stability through false external submission in the political sphere, instead of finding stability through internal submission to rational and revealed truth. Fulton Sheen develops this point as follows:

> When reason cut itself loose from its Divine anchorage, denied absolute truth and reduced everything to a point of view, the field was wide open for propaganda. Minds that were once held together by a common faith or truth were now split into atomic "points of view," waiting for organization and unification.[96]

Such vacuums will be filled by the Hitlers and the Stalins, whose false brands of unity are achieved by way of totalitarian slavery.

Here, as elsewhere, it is in the last analysis only religious truth that sets men free. The papacy, as the infallible voice of that truth, should never be a hindrance or a threat to democracy. It may not be able to declare as normative any one political system, but it can certainly fight its own theocratic temptations. That it has not always done so gives the Vatican grounds for repentance and caution. This, of course, is not a criticism of the Church's authoritative teachings on the moral aspects of political, economic and social problems. If followed during the past half century, these teachings would have saved our war-torn world considerable woe.

The chief freedom necessary to human happiness is freedom from the guilt and destructive consequence of transgression. Our Lord specifically empowered his ambassadors to dispense God's forgiveness and absolution. "Jesus said to them again, 'Peace be with you. As the Father has sent me, even so I send you.' And when he had said this, he breathed on them and said to them, 'Receive the Holy Spirit. If you forgive the sins of any, they are forgiven; if you retain the sins of any, they are retained.' " (John 20:21–23). The Son of God had previously promised that he would give his disciples this power (Matt. 16:18, 18:18), and he now expected them to exercise it in his own name who came to this earth that he might "save his people from their sins" (Matt. 1:21).

"Christ Jesus came into the world to save sinners" (1 Tim. 1:15). On his way through it, he personally, on his own authority (Matt. 9:6), pardoned many flagrant Commandment violators, such as the harlot of the alabaster box (Luke 7:47) and the thief on the cross (Luke 23:43). The absolving work his Father had entrusted to him, the Son of God in his turn entrusted to his apostles.

In order to forgive sins the priest must first learn them: thus the confessional, whose secrecy is inviolable. Warns St. Augustine: "To pretend that it is enough to confess to God alone, is to make void the power of the keys given to the Church, and to contradict the words of Christ in the Gospel."[97]

Confessing personal sins under the seal of secrecy to another human being is the surest way of actually coming to grips with them. Avoidance and repression are so easy where a man is his own judge and jury. It is extremely difficult to be deeply and objectively truthful with one's own failings. As the prophet Jeremiah said: "The heart is deceitful above all things, and desperately corrupt; who can understand it?" (Jer. 17:9). Whether by self-sufficiency, complacency, or self-satisfaction, by censoriousness, ambition, scrupulosity, pretended humility, or pretentiousness—the secretive, short-circuited individual is forever deceiving himself. From these endless varieties of rationalization only an external authority, applying an absolute moral law and a real power of absolution, can ever set men free.

The sacrament of penance is truly a great blessing, for unless a man is free from his sins, all other freedoms are but ornaments on the gown of slavery. From beyond the human frontier, then, through the instrumentality of the priest, when the requirements of contrition and confession have been met, and the penance or prayers have been assigned in satisfaction of the demands of divine justice, then come the emancipating words: "I absolve thee from thy sins in the name of the Father, and of the Son, and of the Holy Spirit." Thus it is that absolution is received, the life of God restored to the soul, and innumerable aids of actual grace bestowed.

Such deep, dynamic freedom of forgiveness, which encourages and warms a man's life like the light of the sun, comes only through captivity to God's truth, which is found in its fullness only in that one Church which he himself founded, who said, "Every one who commits sin is a slave to sin. The slave does not continue in the house for ever, the son continues for ever. So if the Son makes you free, you will be free indeed" (John 8:34–36).

8

Dissolving Difficulties

Catholics worship, in the full sense of the word, a consecrated piece of bread. At the elevation of the host all heads bow in reverent adoration. Is this a form of idolatry, as Protestants often claim, or is this wafer really and truly God Incarnate, Body and Blood, Soul and Divinity, under the appearance of earthly bread? "There is no more blatant idolatry in all heathendom than the idolatry of the mass. So, then, the very heart of the whole Roman system is a great blasphemy."[98] This statement would quite obviously be true if the doctrine of transubstantiation were false.

There is no middle ground. Either Jesus Christ is actually present in the Holy Eucharist or he is not. Either Protestantism or Catholicism is drastically wrong on this central issue.

There have been over two hundred different interpretations of those four plain and simple words: "This is my body" (Matt. 26:26; Mark 14:22; Luke 22:19; I Cor. 11:24). Since the sixteenth century Protestantism has divided and subdivided over the proper method of explaining away their literal meaning. But at the present time three-fourths of the world's Christians still accept the straightforward Catholic interpretation of those words.

The Roman Church, as can be ascertained by historical investigation, has never varied in its firm belief that by God's express will the priestly words of consecration actually change bread and wine into the Body and Blood of Christ. The Council of Trent defined this doctrine against the Protestant Reformers as follows:

> The Holy Synod teaches . . . that in the august Sacrament of the Holy Eucharist, after the consecration of the bread and wine, our Lord Jesus Christ, true God and Man, is truly, really and substan-

tially contained under the appearance of those sensible things. . . . If anyone denies that in the Sacrament of the most Holy Eucharist are contained truly, really and substantially the Body and Blood, together with the Soul and Divinity of our Lord Jesus Christ, and consequently the whole Christ; but says that he is therein only as a sign, or a figure or virtually, let him be anathema.

Looking back to the Fathers of the early Church, we find them using many expressions to signify this change, which has aptly and accurately been called Transubstantiation. They say the elements "pass into," "become," "are made," or "trans-elemented into" the Body and Blood of our Lord, thus signifying their conviction that while the visible elements of bread and wine retain their surface appearance, the inner reality is radically altered in kind from a non-living substance to a living one.

St. John Chrysostom (died 407) writes:

If you were indeed incorporeal, he would have delivered to you those same incorporeal gifts without covering. But since the soul is united to the body, he delivers to you in things perceptible to the senses the things to be apprehended by the understanding. How many nowadays say: "Would that they could look upon his [Jesus'] form, his figure, his raiment, his shoes." Lo! you see him, touch him, eat him.

St. Ambrose (died 391) writes:

Of the works of the whole world thou hast read: He spoke and they were made. Cannot, then, the word of Christ which was able to make out of nothing that which was not, change the things which are into that which they were not?

St. Justin Martyr (died 165) writes:

We do not receive these things as common bread and drink; but as Jesus Christ our Savior was made flesh by the word of God, even so we have been taught that the Eucharist is both the flesh and the blood of the same Incarnate Jesus.

St. Ignatius of Antioch (died 107) says of heretics that they "abstain from the Eucharist and prayer, because they confess not that the Eucharist is the flesh of our Savior Jesus Christ, the flesh which suffered for our sins, which the Father in his mercy raised up."

St. Paul of Tarsus, witnessing to the faith of the apostolic Church, says that the effect of Holy Communion is to make the partakers, who are many, into one body (1 Cor. 11:17), and immediately thereafter he calls this one body "the body of Christ" (1 Cor. 12:17). He testifies to the fact that he has received a special revelation on this one teaching, follows this with the words of institution, and then warns against the crime of blasphemous communion, for which cause "many of you are weak and ill, and some have died" (1 Cor. 11:23–30). This crime is committed by that man who "eats and drinks without discerning the body, [who] eats and drinks judgment upon himself." How could St. Paul say more clearly that Christ was truly present? Could one possibly be "guilty of the body and blood of the Lord" through unworthy, undiscerning communion if he were eating ordinary bread and drinking ordinary wine? Would not God be a monster to damn anyone for dishonoring the mere elements of nature? Symbolic interpretation makes nonsense of these words; only the doctrine of the Real Presence reflects their self-evident meaning. "Take, eat: this *is* my body."

Our Lord was nearing the cross when he spoke these words of institution. The clarity and simplicity of approaching death are upon them, the straightforwardness of a last will and testament which the author desires no man to misunderstand or misinterpret. This Last Supper was a meal of final parting. At such a time promises and commands are not given in metaphorical, figurative, or symbolical language. Men at the point of death speak to be surely understood.

Jesus never suggested that his words needed any spiritualizing interpretation or explaining away. Neither did Matthew, Mark, Luke, or Paul, who amply corroborate each other's records on this subject (Matt. 26:26–28; Mark 14:22–24; Luke 22:19–20; 1 Cor. 11:23–25). John writes at length, immediately after the miracles of the multiplication of the loaves and fishes, telling of our Lord's advance promise of the Eucharist, which his words and actions at the Last Supper fulfilled. He warns that his words cannot rightly be understood by the mere carnal mind, but only by the spirit-led mind (John 6:63–65: compare use of "flesh" and "spirit" here with Matt. 26:41, John 3:6, and Rom. 8:6–9). Many even among his disciples found the following "a hard saying" and "walked no more with him"—" 'I am the living bread which came down from heaven; if any one eats of this bread, he will live for ever; and the bread which I shall give for the life of the world is my flesh.' The Jews then disputed among themselves, saying, 'How can this man give us his flesh to eat?' So Jesus said to them, 'Truly, truly, I say to you, unless you eat the flesh of the Son of man and drink his blood, you have no life in you; he who eats my flesh and drinks my blood has eternal life, and I will raise him up at the last day. For my flesh is food indeed, and my blood is drink indeed. He who eats my flesh and drinks my blood abides in me, and I in him. As the living Father sent me, and I live because of the Father, so he who eats me will live because of me. This is the bread which came down from heaven, not such as the fathers ate and died; he who eats this bread will live for ever' " (John 6:51–58).

But how can this food be so superior to the ancient manna that it will produce eternal life, if it be only natural, earthly bread and nothing more? Mere commemorative food and drink would be inferior to the miraculous manna which God showered upon the journeying Israelites (Ex. 16:14–15).

Since the God-man himself has declared so clearly, *This is my Body*, what mere human being—in his sin and ignorance—will dare to doubt, deny, and contradict him, saying, *This is not his body?*

> *Credo quidquid dixit Dei Filius*
> *Nil hoc veritatis verbo verius.*

> What God's own Son has spoken is my creed:
> No truer word than his, who is the Truth indeed.[99]

Other difficult Roman doctrines, in a like manner, lose their seeming extravagance and incredibility when through open-minded investigation the clear light of reason shines upon them.

The doctrine of indulgences, for example, has often been grossly misunderstood by its critics. It has nothing whatsoever to do with either the forgiveness or permission of sin. An indulgence is a remission of the temporal punishment due to sin *after its guilt has been contritely confessed and forgiven.*

Every sin carries in its wake penalties to be undergone both here and hereafter. The eternal punishment of hell (due to any unrepented mortal or grievous sin, which by its very nature is an infinite offense against God's purity) is always remitted in a good confession. But when contrition is imperfect, temporal punishment may still remain—that is, God may allow the soul to make up in suffering what it lacked in sorrow.

In God's plan a virtuous act, because it is based on love of God, wins reward[100] and thereby diminishes the debt of this temporal punishment for past sins. Salvation, of course, depends completely upon Christ, for only he could pay the debt of even one mortal sin. But the individual can co-operate *in* Christ on his own behalf through deeds of penance and virtue.

The doctrine of indulgences presupposes the belief that the virtuous acts of one man can help to pay the debt of his brother. If this were not so, our Lord could not save us by the merits of his earthly works and atoning death, however infinite their value. God's justice must be satisfied: he cannot abrogate it and still remain true to his own nature. That Jesus paid the penalty for us, Christians agree, and this presupposes the principle of vicarious satisfaction.

Members of Christ are one body: when one suffers, all suffer; when one regains lost health, other parts of the body are thereby benefited. Individual human beings in the Church are not separate, lonely atoms, but mutually dependent organs of a single living organism, the Mystical Body of Christ. The communion of saints is a spiritual union, joining by muscular sinew, nervous system and bloodstream, as it were, all the faithful, whether on earth or beyond. This is the divine kingdom of God, permeated by his supernatural life, embracing all the elect, who are united in the bonds of charity and by a desire to work, suffer, and pray for each other. As Paul says: "We, though many, are one body in Christ, and individually members one of another" (Rom. 12:5). In our own day Sigrid Undset writes:

> This is the communism of the society of the blessed: just as the rewards of the blessed are collected in the treasurehouse of the Church, so that every poor and infirm soul may have its share of this treasure, so in a mysterious way the sins of the faithful impoverish the whole of Christendom. Our generation, which has seen how the horrors of war and the concentration camps have fallen alike on the guilty and on those who by human reckoning were the most guiltless, should find it easier than our forefathers, with their naive belief in personal success as a reward for personal service, to understand the dogma of the Church that we all have our share in the rewards of all the saints and the guilt of all sinners.[101]

Thus it is, through the oneness of the communion of saints and through the principle of vicarious satisfaction, that the inexhaustible supply of merit gained by Christ, and secondarily by his saints, is able to pay the debts of poorer brethren. In the Church all things are held in common, including the merit and reward of the virtuous acts of its members. These constitute a great "common stock" treasury, to which the saints in their heroism are able to add by a superabundance of good works. Thus St. Paul rejoices even in his extreme sufferings, which "complete what is lacking in Christ's afflictions for the sake of his body, that is, the church" (Col. 1:24). And St. Thomas Aquinas, glorious Doctor and Teacher of the faithful, says this: "All the saints intended that whatever they did or suffered for God's sake should be profitable not only to themselves but to the whole Church."

This great treasure of vicarious satisfaction our Lord entrusted to St. Peter and his successors when he said: "I will give you the keys of the kingdom of heaven, and whatever you bind on earth shall be bound in heaven, and whatever you loose on earth shall be loosed in heaven" (Matt. 16:19). The pope exercises this power when he attaches to certain prayers or acts an indulgence of so many days or years (time-quantities are a survival of the length of the ancient harsher penalties imposed by the Church on sinners, which now are replaced by certain prayers and prescribed acts).

Thus does the chief ruler of the Church beg God to remit, in part or in whole, by virtue of the merits of Christ and his saints, the temporal punishment due to sin. And because in Christ all are one, God accepts this vicarious payment of love just as if the sinner himself had satisfied the demands of eternal justice.

Such an indulgence, or remission of temporal penalty, may be gained only after repentance and a good confession have removed the sin's guilt, and when the purpose of amendment and the willingness to do penance are sincerely present.

Since those suffering purification after death are members of the communion of saints, the faithful on earth can pray that God will apply such indulgences as they have gained to these other souls in purgatory. They are applied only by way of intercession, and God alone can determine their effectiveness, but what a joy and hope this teaching can be to Catholics, who feel that they are thus able to do something definite for those who have gone beyond. If the request for the shortening of time in purgatory is in accordance with the heavenly Father's will, such an indulgence will be applied by him as he sees fit. There is no question here of God's compromising his justice, for we are members of one Body, and it is right that the strength of one should help the weakness of another. Such remission or shortening of the remedial punishments of purgatory is beyond the Church's authoritative jurisdiction, but not beyond her concern, suffrage, and intercession.

Now it is true that there have been abuses and perversions of this teaching, as there have been, at one time or another in the Church's long history, misusages of most other teachings. But an abuse of a truth does not invalidate or repeal the truth itself. When unscrupulous men torture and twist some doctrine for their own material gain, this in no sense falsifies the pure doctrine itself. "It is necessary that temptations come," said our Lord, "but woe to the man by whom the temptation comes!" (Matt. 18:7).

Because they do not understand all this, some non-Catholics often misrepresent Catholic practice most seriously. Masses for the dead, to illustrate, may not be sold for money, and so it is a gross falsehood to say: "Oh that poor Catholic girl buys a Mass for her poor dead father every week—no wonder she hasn't got enough money for lunch!" It may well be that she does not eat lunch because the season is Lent and she is fasting, a salutary practice often recommended by our Lord (Matt. 4:2, 6:16, 9:15) and his apostles (Acts 13:2; 2 Cor. 11:27; Gal. 5:24). In any event, Masses in themselves cannot be bought, since the Church's Canon Law forbids simony, which it defines as "a deliberate eagerness to buy or sell for a temporal price anything intrinsically spiritual."[102] It is true that in connection with saying the Mass the priest accepts a fixed stipend for his support for the day and other expenses incidental to the Mass, but this is not the price of the Mass any more than the money which a Protestant gives for a Bible is the price of the word of God. Furthermore, the priest is usually quite willing to say a Mass without stipend if requested to do so for a good reason.

Nor is it true that Catholics believe the sacrifice of the Mass to be a repetition of the one all-sufficient sacrifice at Calvary. These two sacrifices are in reality one and identical. The Mass is the means instituted by God whereby the sole and unrepeatable immolation of Calvary is here and now made present for us, offered up on our behalf, and thus applied to our present individual needs.

As in the case of indulgences, when a Mass is said for a soul who might be suffering in purgatory, this is done not by way of jurisdiction, but by way of intercession and in full realization that the potential and particular application of the infinite merits of the sacrifice of the cross are completely in God's hands—as indeed also is the eternal destiny of each and every soul at the moment of death.

The Church is unable to judge whether this or that individual has gone to hell, purgatory, or heaven. Not even the priest who hears the deathbed confession and administers the last rites can tell for certain. This destiny depends on the true inner state of the soul, which is known only to God.

The Church does, however, define quite clearly the conditions requisite for entry into hell, purgatory, and heaven. After the death of the physical body, the soul with its faculties of intellect, will, and memory continues in perfect consciousness as it enters into an exclusively spiritual state of being. Once in life, a soul never ceases to exist, though by reason of mortal sin and the subsequent loss of sanctifying grace, it can lose God forever.

At the moment of death each soul is confronted by God in particular judgment and receives an eternal reward or punishment, which thenceforth is irreversible. There is no second chance. In this mortal life God offers all men sufficient grace to save their immortal souls. "Behold, now is the acceptable time; behold, now is the day of salvation" (2 Cor. 6:2).

Those who have never heard the name of Jesus nor received the fullness of his revelation are judged by the amount of light they have received. An unbaptized pagan who believes in God and his rewarding Providence (Heb. 11:6) and who has followed the natural law will by God's grace be saved just as surely as the good Catholic; for though he is not a member of the body of the Church, he is part of her soul by virtue of faith in God and firm adherence to the highest truth he has known.

The loss of God, the slavery of Satan, the torments of hell—these are the lot of those who die in mortal sin, having on their consciences unrepented and grievous offenses against the law of God. Such is the clear and obvious teaching of Jesus Christ, who is God and therefore cannot deceive. It is his desire and purpose that all men should be saved, and yet he has given his creatures free will and the possibility of continuing to misuse this free will to the very end. Those who are finally disobedient and impenitent exclude themselves forever from the Joyous Home, entering instead into a place of everlasting pain, regret, and self-hatred, where "their worm shall not die, their fire shall not be quenched" (Isa. 66:24). Page after page of the New Testament teaches the reality of such eternal damnation for the wicked and impenitent (Matt. 3:12; 7:21-23; 13:30, 49-50; 22:13; 25:11-12, 30, 41, 46). The denial of such

> an ultimate sanction would lead to the absurd statement that a man might blaspheme and hate God, and fling up to heaven his deliberate preference of some loathsome pleasure to the possession of him, and that he might do so with the calm certainty that God was bound to forgive him. Thus God would betray helplessness towards his own creatures.[103]

At the moment of death, when the will is fixed forever, many souls are fit for neither heaven nor hell. They are not in a state of mortal sin, yet they are defiled by smaller faults for which remedial punishment is still due. These enter into a place of purification known as purgatory, fully assured that when their debt has been paid they will join the blessed in heaven. They are completely reconciled to the will of God. They recognize the necessity and justice of the painful fires, which burn away their dross of character. They even rejoice in this tribulation, knowing that it works for them "an eternal weight of glory" (2 Cor. 4:17).

The soul which is in any way defiled cannot enter God's presence (Rev. 21:27), for he is "of purer eyes than to behold evil/ and canst not look on wrong" (Hab. 1:13). Such souls are saved only by a cleansing fire. Though they "will never get out" till they have "paid the last penny" (Matt. 5:26), the prayers of those on earth and in heaven help them in their suffering. "It was a holy and pious thought. Therefore he made atonement for the dead, that they might be delivered from their sin" (2 Macc. 12:45).

Under the Old Law many Jews believed in praying for their dead, and our divine Lord, who regularly attended synagogue and temple services, never once condemned or corrected them for this practice. Since he often denounced the corruptions introduced by the scribes and Pharisees, his silence on this score entitles Christians to continue the custom as a true and lawful form of intercession, which is able to give genuine aid and comfort to the suffering souls in purgatory.

Requiem eternam dona eis, Domine,
Et lux perpetua luceat eis!
Requiescant in pace!
Amen!

Such has been the teaching of the Church down the ages, from the catacombs and early Fathers to the present day. Upon careful and unbiased examination the truth-seeking Christian will surely find that

Rome's conception of purgatory is the only logical and unassailable one, and here is the only doctrine that fits in, not only with Scripture and tradition, but even with reason and commonsense. Her teaching on this, as on all other dogmas of the faith, is clear, intelligible, and precise, whilst the opinions of heretics are nebulous, confused, and contradictory, in conflict at once with a true philosophy of man's nature and the theology revealed by Jesus Christ.[104]

The souls in purgatory undergo their sufferings in a spirit of hope and joy. Death cannot limit the power of Christ's blood to reach across the grave and cleanse them. They know that the full happiness of the beatific vision will eventually be theirs. Face to face and unashamed, they too shall see their Savior and all his holy angels, along with saints and apostles, kindred and friends of old, in that blessed realm called heaven, where all difficulties are at last dissolved.

9

Theotokos

Four-fifths of the world's Christians recognize Mary as *Theotokos*, or Mother of God, and in daily requests for her intercessory prayer, call her blessed, who under the inspiration of the Holy Spirit predicted: "All generations will call me blessed" (Luke 1:48). Protestants, for the most part, ignore Mary while accusing the four-fifths who honor her of Mariolatry, that is, of worshiping Mary as a god and of setting Christ aside in her favor. Which of these two positions reflects the truth? Which has the mind of Mary's divine Son?

Mary herself had that true mark of saintliness, humility. She appears infrequently throughout the gospels, and this has been attributed to her retiring and reticent nature. She kept unspoken many of the deeper mysteries of the Incarnation. St. Luke, who must have interviewed her on this subject, twice tells that she kept many things to herself and pondered them in her heart (Luke 2:19, 51). What ineffable mysteries must have been contemplated in the mind of her whose body was "the chosen vessel wherein the union of Godhood and manhood had taken place."[105] What refreshing lights must secretly have descended upon the inward eye of her adoring gaze!

Yet she called herself God's "handmaiden" of "low estate" and "low degree." In self-forgetfulness she magnified the Lord, who had sent his high angel to her with this message: " 'Hail, full of grace, the Lord is with you!' . . . 'Do not be afraid, Mary, for you have found favor with God' " (Luke 1:28, 30). The angelic messenger asks this young Jewish girl if she of her own free will agrees to give the Second Person of the Holy Trinity a human nature. Mary is troubled as to how this shall come about in her virginity. The angel assures her that God himself will work the necessary miracle of divine paternity. Humbly she gives her consent: "Behold, I am the handmaid of the Lord; let it be to me according to your word" (Luke 1:38).

Thus it was that Almighty God took human flesh from a Jewish maid. That flesh had to be free from the least taint of original sin if our Lord was to be without reproach. "Had Infinite Purity chosen any other port of entrance into humanity but that of human purity, it would have created a tremendous difficulty—namely, how could he be sinless, if he was born of sin-laden humanity?"[106] The Catholic Church teaches that Mary was indeed set apart from all other mothers or "blessed among women," "full of grace," and "highly favored," never under the influence of Satan, never displeasing to God from the very first moment of her existence. For God the Son from eternity willed at the instant her soul was created that all the merits of his passion, crucifixion, and death be applied to her in advance, just as these merits are now applied to other mortals in the sacrament of baptism. Thus by an "immaculate conception" he fashioned for himself a worthy mother, a perfect creature, through whom to enter this sinful world. Having thus created her pure and holy, by the gift of special graces he enabled her to remain untouched by sin throughout her entire earthly life.

Who, being God, would do less for his own mother? Who can suppose that the one woman whose vocation it was to give God the flesh and blood with which he would redeem the whole world would herself be under the curse of original sin, without God's grace in her soul? Yet most Protestant leaders go on maintaining that Mary was a sinner like other human beings, begrudging her the special protective graces which God gave her throughout her earthly life. It is difficult to understand how anyone can hope to please Jesus Christ by ignoring or disparaging his holy mother. Certainly the early Protestant Reformers were as anti-Nestorian as the Council of Ephesus, which declared in 431 that Mary was indeed entitled to the designation "Mother of God." John

Calvin writes: "We cannot acknowledge the blessings brought us by Jesus without acknowledging at the same time how highly God honored and enriched Mary in choosing her for the Mother of God."[107] This, of course, does not mean that Mary brought our Lord's divine nature into existence, nor did she pre-exist him as ordinary mothers pre-exist their children. The title *Theotokos* signifies that she gave human flesh to the Second Person of the Blessed Trinity, and thus became the Mother of God-become-Man.

As such, she fed the Author of Life upon her breast. She taught him his first baby words and provided his first model of behavior. As a young boy, he was voluntarily subject to her (Luke 2:51). He spent the first thirty years of his human life in her daily company. He worked his first miracle at her request (John 2:1–11). What honor can be too great to ascribe to such a chosen woman?

> She is more than a minor accessory in the working out of the divine plan, whose usefulness can be quickly recognized and then dropped out of sight and disregarded. Almighty God did not honor her by making her the mother of the Second Person of the Blessed Trinity without expecting that we should likewise honor her.[108]

Those who invoke her prayers in the traditional *Ave Maria* do just that when they say: "Holy Mary, Mother of God, pray for us sinners now and at the hour of our death. Amen."

How can anyone believe that God, who thus honored Mary, would ever harshly rebuke her? When he replied to a compliment given his mother by saying: "Blessed rather are those who hear the word of God and keep it" (Luke 11:28), he was simply stating the fact that spiritual ties run deeper than the ties of flesh and blood. Catholics today are closer to Christ by grace than ever Mary was by the deed of natural birth and physical motherhood. Mary herself did undoubtedly "hear the word of God and keep it" as well as any of the saints. There is no rebuke to her in this teaching. Nor is there in the saying: "My mother and my brethren are those who hear the word of God and do it" (Luke 8:21). If there was any rebuke involved, it was meant for his worldly "hearers" upon that occasion. How unlikely it is that he who gave the law, "Honor your father and your mother" (Ex. 20:12), would purposely break that law when he became a man!

Since the fifth century among the Greeks and the sixth century among the Latins, the feast of the Assumption has been observed in Christendom. It must have been preached continuously for centuries before that in order to receive such uncontested, worldwide acknowledgment and affirmation. In the fourth century St. Gregory of Tours wrote: "The Lord had the most holy body of the Virgin taken into heaven, where, reunited to her soul, it now enjoys, with the elect, happiness without end."[109] Early in the next century St. Modestus, Patriarch of Jerusalem, preached on the Feast of the Falling Asleep of Mary:

> O most blessed Dormition of the glorious Mother of God, always a virgin, who never knew the decay of the sepulcher because our almighty Savior Jesus Christ kept intact the flesh of which he was born. . . . The most glorious mother of Christ our Savior and our God, who gives life and immortality, was raised again by him, shares incorruption with him for all ages—with him who reclaimed her from the tomb and took her to himself, as he himself knows, to whom be glory and empire with the Father and the Holy Spirit forever.[110]

This belief in the Assumption has been explicitly held by the vast majority of Christians over the intervening centuries, and according to the formula of St. Augustine, *securus judicat orbis terrarum*, the whole world judges safely. Since Christ has promised that the Church would not go astray into the ways of death (Matt. 16:18), but that on the contrary, his Holy Spirit would lead it at the proper time into the explicit definition of all necessary truth (John 16:13), the four-fifths of Christendom which thus honors Mary could not possibly be wrong.

The Church never claimed to be in possession of the relics and remains of our Lord's mother, for it knew that soon after Mary's death her physical body was resurrected by divine power and taken up into heaven, because of her perpetual immunity from sin and by virtue of her close union with God's only Son. As Pope Pius XII explained in his official *ex cathedra* proclamation:

> We must remember especially that, since the second century, the Virgin Mary has been designated by the Holy Fathers as the new Eve, who, although subject to the new Adam, is most intimately associated with him in that struggle against the infernal foe which, as foretold in the protoevangelium (Gen. 3:15), finally resulted in that most complete victory over the sin and death which are always mentioned together in the writings of the Apostle of the Gentiles (cf. Rom. Chapters 5 and 6). Consequently, just as the glorious Resurrection of Christ was an essential part and final sign of this victory, so that struggle which was common to the Blessed Virgin and her divine Son should be brought to a close by the glorification of her virginal body.[111]

In heaven Mary has been exalted as Queen of all creatures, whether human or angelic, for no other created being was ever privileged to participate so closely in the mediation of God's salvation to the world. She does not cause grace: that power belongs to Christ alone. But she who freely consented to provide God with that human flesh which would serve to redeem innumerable lost sinners became by that deed a secondary mediatrix of all his graces. Secondary because her mediation is "*in* Christ, not . . . *in addition to Christ.*"[112] Now in heaven she continues to co-operate, though only through her prayers, in the work of bringing her Son to birth again and again within countless souls of the Church Militant upon earth. She who has been called "the Accomplice of the Incarnation" is also God's indirect accomplice in the extension of his Incarnation through the new birth described in the third chapter of John's gospel. In this birth, too, Mary has an indispensable, though external, part to play. The faithful summon her prayers ceaselessly, as they may also request the prayers of their own earthly mothers. If Christians here upon earth, by praying for each other, can become secondary mediators of God's blessing, how much more, then, is Mary to be acknowledged as the Mediatrix of All Graces, who gives her Son and her prayers for all.

If Christians on earth are members of Christ's body (Rom. 12:5, 1 Cor. 12:27), then we can see why Mary who gave that body to the world was made by Christ to be the spiritual mother of all the members of that mystical fellowship. Our Blessed Lord, Catholics believe, proclaimed this truth about our Blessed Mother when from the height of Calvary's cross he said to Mary concerning the disciple whom he loved: "Woman, behold, your son"; and then to St. John: "Behold, your mother" (John 19:26–27). God has truly given this universal mother a great work to do. And yet, as John Henry Newman explains:

> Mary is only our Mother by divine appointment, given us from the Cross; her presence is above, not on earth; her office is external, not within us. Her name is not heard in the administration of the Sacraments. Her work is not one of ministration towards us; her power is indirect. It is her prayers that avail, and her prayers are effectual by the will of Him who is our all in all. Nor need she hear us by any innate power or personal gift; but by His manifestation to her of the prayers which we make to her. When Moses was on the Mount, the Almighty told him of the idolatry of his people at the foot of it, in order that he might intercede for them; and thus it is the Divine Presence which is the intermediating Power by which we reach her and she reaches us.[113]

Our Lady Mary can in no sense be said to supplant or displace our Lord Christ, "who is God over all, blessed for ever" (Rom. 9:5). Even if it were possible, which it is not, she would never desire such a treachery. She who gave Christ to all souls would never take a single soul from him. If she were capable of such a deviltry, the Church would renounce her! But humbly she leads sinners to him and begs his graces upon them. It is impossible to honor Mary too highly so long as she is not deified. And Catholics definitely do not adore her, as if she were a goddess, or offer her divine homage, but only veneration and high reverence. The famous English convert, Frederick Faber, author of hymns so well-known to Protestants as "Faith of Our Fathers" and "There's a Wideness in God's Mercy," gave this heartfelt answer to former

Protestant friends who misinterpreted his new-found devotion to
the Blessed Virgin:

> But scornful men have coldly said
> Thy love was leading me from God;
> And yet in this I did but tread
> The very path my Savior trod.
> They know but little of thy worth,
> Who speak these heartless words to me.
> For what did Jesus love on earth
> One-half so tenderly as thee?

Now in heaven this limitless love for his mother continues un-
abated, as together they work co-operatively in the great task of
intercession for the saving of our recalcitrant world. The pure human nature which Mary gave her divine Son has been exalted to
the right hand of God the Father Almighty, while her own spiritu-
alized body, from which his was born, has also been taken up into
heaven. Were it any wonder, then, if God the Son should have
seen fit in recent years to trust his mother and ours with missions
of the utmost importance to the modern world? Would it not be
appropriate that this one sinless-yet-merely-human creature, "our
tainted nature's solitary boast," should have been sent by Christ
to plead with a world of sinners that they repent and return to
God?

This is exactly what happened in 1830 at the Rue du Bac in
Paris, in 1846 on the mountain fields of La Salette, in 1858 at
Lourdes, and in 1917 at Fatima. No Catholic is bound to believe
in any of these visitations, but the vast majority do. They believe
that on behalf of her divine Son, and on behalf of sinners, the
Blessed Virgin visited this sick old earth with urgent warnings of
crisis and calamity to come if her requests for prayers and penance
were ignored and people did not cease offending Almighty God.
She offered new means of blessing and shed healing graces upon
many. She asked for humility through regular contemplation of
the mysteries of the Rosary (whose ordered prayers are scorned by
the proud but valued by the lowly who alone know their worth).

She told the children at Fatima: "When you say the rosary, say at the end of each mystery: 'O my Jesus, forgive us. Preserve us from the fire of hell. Take all souls to heaven, and help especially those most in need.' "

In Paris in 1830, Catherine Labouré, a simple, hard-working peasant girl who had recently become a postulant with the Sisters of Charity, was awakened from her sleep one July night and led to the seminary chapel by a radiant child. She confessed later: "I believe the child was my guardian angel, because I had always prayed to him for the favor of seeing the Blessed Virgin." When she appeared, our Lady said to Catherine: "I have a mission to entrust to you. You will have much to suffer in its performance, but the thought that it will be for the glory of God will enable you to overcome all trials. You will be opposed, but do not be afraid. Grace will be given to you."[114] God's grace permeated Catherine Labouré, body and soul, to such an extent that when her body was exhumed in 1933, fifty-seven years after her death, it was found to be incorrupt, and in 1947 her soul was declared to be in heaven—that is, she was proclaimed a saint by Pope Pius XII.

Mélanie and Maximin, the children of La Salette, also had to suffer for the apparition they saw as they tended their cows on the mountain pasturelands. Yet five years after the Blessed Virgin had spoken with them, an episcopal letter was read in the six hundred churches of the Grenoble diocese:

> We declare that the apparition of the Blessed Virgin to the two shepherds, on September 19, 1846, on a mountain in the Alps in the parish of La Salette, bears in itself all the marks of truth and that the faithful are justified in believing without question in its truth. And so, to mark our lively gratitude to God and the glorious Virgin Mary, we authorize the cult of Our Lady of La Salette.[115]

Such a verdict is only given after rigorous and lengthy examination of all the evidence involved.

The story of Bernadette Soubirous and the miracle of Lourdes is known the world over. So too are Lucia, Francisco, and Jacinta, the children of Fatima, who many months in advance prophesied that terrifying miracle which was seen at noon of October 13, 1917, near Lisbon, Portugal, by seventy thousand concurring witnesses! A few days later the Communist revolution triumphed in Russia, thereby giving increased emphasis to our Lady's words: "If my request is heard, Russia will be converted and there will be peace. If not, Russia will spread her errors throughout the world, causing wars and persecutions of the Church."

Impartial examination of the evidence has led countless people of high intelligence to the acceptance of the reality of these apparitions. But their authenticity is not a dogma of the Church, and it is not necessary to believe in these visitations of the Blessed Virgin in order to become a Catholic. However, canonical investigations are detailed and thorough, and not many of the faithful would doubt the validity of their final verdicts.

After all, Mary *is* the Mother of God, the queen of heaven and earth: great actions can well be expected of her in such decisive and perilous times as these.

10

Bless the Heretics!

Many saintly heretics, who never lost the grace God gave them at baptism, shine forth from the pages of Protestant history. Rome has not cornered the market on outstanding virtue, persistent prayer, and heroic self-denial. Yet the holiness of these sincere heretics has been gained in spite of their errors and not because of them.

"Love men; hate error," said Augustine sixteen centuries ago. Our Lord's modern disciples can follow no better advice. Far from there being any degree of intolerance in hating falsehood, it is the plain duty of every rational creature; it is the reverse side of the lust for truth, a virtue enjoined by God Incarnate when he said: "For this I was born, and for this I have come into the world, to bear witness to the truth. Every one who is of the truth hears my voice" (John 18:37). But what of those who through no fault of their own have never really heard that voice?

In his infinite mercy may Almighty God bountifully bless all such pagans, heretics, and schismatics by leading them back to the One, Holy, Catholic, and Apostolic Church! May the hidden work of his grace turn their hearts in that far country from the husks and famine of error to the feast that awaits them in their Father's home! And when at last they have found his truth, may he give them courage to follow where it leads!

Abraham, prime patriarch and father of all the faithful, when he had seen the vision of the city of God (Heb. 11:10), displayed such courage. The Lord had said to him: "Go from your country . . . to the land that I will show you . . . and I will bless you . . . so that you will be a blessing" (Gen. 12:1–2). In response to this divine command he left behind forever the strange gods of his fathers and their seductive ways of life. It was not easy for him to pull up all his roots and move on, but a supernal inner voice summoned him to the fulfilling of his destiny, and he saw quite clearly that his choice was between everlasting reward and everlasting remorse. "By faith Abraham obeyed when he was called to go out to a place which he was to receive as an inheritance" (Heb. 11:8). On this earth Abraham never found the promised city of God, but he saw it from afar, and for this vision of future blessing he forsook all and followed after the one true God.

How much more readily should that man answer the divine call who with his own eyes has seen the city set on a hill, which is the one true Church of Christ, whose builder and maker is God. Let him not delay unduly once the Spirit of certitude has taken hold of him. Nor let him say within himself: "But I am already in the line of salvation with Abraham as my father." For when those whom God has called do not answer, he is able to raise up from the very stones of the earth "children to Abraham" (Matt. 3:9).

God is good. He is long-suffering and patient toward the sons of men, "not wishing that any should perish" (2 Pet. 3:9). On the contrary, he "desires all men to be saved and to come to knowledge of the truth" (1 Tim. 2:4). When he visited this earth long ago in the flesh and bones of a human creature, he founded a divine society which he promised would never fail nor fall into error (Matt. 16:18–19), because it would be protected by his own very real Presence until the end of time (Matt. 28:20). He ordered the clergy of this Society, or Church, to teach with his own authority all those truths which his Holy Spirit would bring to their remembrance (John 14:26, 16:13).

Protestant and other innovators accuse this Church of teaching falsehood and of falling into corruption through prevalence of the powers of death. But this is exactly what our Lord guaranteed would never happen! Whom, then, are searching souls to believe and follow—the sincere-but-deceived children of chaos, or the one true God and his one true Church? Everlasting reward and everlasting remorse may hang in the balance of this choice.

God is good. "His mercy is on those who fear him from generation to generation." He speaks today "as he spoke to our fathers, to Abraham and to his posterity for ever" (Luke 1:50, 55). Above the indecision of the inner debate, the clarion call of the eternal sounds forth once again (Gen. 12:1; Luke 18:29–30)— "Go from your country and your kindred and your father's house to the land that I will show you." . . . "There is no man who has left house or wife or brothers or parents or children, for the sake of the kingdom of God, who will not receive manifold more in this time, and in the age to come eternal life."

Note of Appreciation

Today I have been reading the galley proofs of this manuscript, which has been out of my hands for a full half year. How amazed I am to find so little mention of that which now means more to me than all else in my religion—the Holy Eucharist, the Blessed Sacrament. How much I still have to learn about the faith!

Many thanks to my wife and Mr. F. J. Sheed, the Catholic layman of the 12 November 1954 entry, for their valuable criticisms and suggestions. May God richly bless all the angelic host at Sheed & Ward, Inc., for the care which they are giving to the preparation of this book.

Through the mysterious workings of the Holy Spirit my wife's inner conversion of belief came about in mid-February 1955. On March 14 in New York City, she met Mr. and Mrs. F. J. Sheed and Rev. John F. McConnell, M.M., the first three people to know of our intention to join the Church. The priest with whom Marjorie and I earlier considered the possibility was Rev. William McNaughton of the 10 May 1954 entry, a Maryknoll Missioner now in Korea.

We also wish to thank Rev. Mother Benedict, the nuns and priest—Rev. Theodore Beauchamp—at Regina Laudis Abbey for introducing us to the Benedictine way of life, for giving us a home and instruction in the faith during the spring of 1955.

We recall with gratitude those many kind and generous souls who sought to aid our search for a new way of life, most especially Mr. Sheed, Reverend Mother Columba of the Maryknoll Sisters, Rev. Joseph McSorley of the Paulist Fathers, and Rev. James Keller of the Christophers.

Though strongly Protestant in their faith, our parents have helped us in countless ways: to them we owe our greatest debt of gratitude. May the light of God's love shine in them, and through them, and round about them, now and ever.

For these and all the blessings of a merciful Providence, we say again and again "Deo gratias."

OLIVER BARRES, JR.
12 November 1955

Afterword

With a Jubilee year our twentieth century is mercifully expiring. It has been a cauldron of nuclear perils, racial pogroms, and renascent paganism. Idols have been widely worshipped, dark powers masquerading as truth. In 1923, shortly after a roaring decade and I were born, T. S. Eliot described our times as an "immense panorama of futility and anarchy" without a unifying principle. People have forgotten what life is about because they have forgotten the City of God, and our secular world, having lost a sense of the supernatural, is dying of spiritual drought. Without God's help man alone is incapable of comprehending reality and structuring his existence accordingly. When he tries by himself to build a better world, he soon finds out that the temporal order as an end in itself is a dead end.

The only real answer to the human predicament was given long ago to the apostles, priests, and people of the Catholic Church. Today, it's all there in the declarations of Vatican Council II, in John Paul II's new *Catechism*, and his diagnostic encyclicals, such as *The Mercy of God*. The plan of God is to raise men and women to a participation in his own divine life: to accomplish this he has made Christ the source of salvation for the whole world. Unfortunately, a majority of the human race does not know or believe this. As the fourth book of the New Testament puts it: "He was in the world, and the world was made through him, yet the world knew him not" (John 1:10). As Christians, we pray for the birth of a new day in which all will see with new eyes the One who said, "I am the light of the world; he who follows me will not walk in darkness" (John 8:12).

Seeing the Light

It took Marjorie and me a long time to see the light that never wanes. This book tells you how it happened and what happened to us since, along with our thoughts on the present state of the Church. The *Afterword* you are reading also sketches in our prior lives and some earlier experiences that influenced our conversion: you'll know where the book came from. Its first publication in 1956 was accompanied by the prayers of a great many sisters and brothers, priests and lay people, prayers especially for the searching souls who would read it looking for lasting help. These prayers, I believe, are still operative. New ones from many quarters hover in the background.

Marjorie and I read many conversion stories as we considered the claims of the Catholic Church. All were written after the fact —helpful but looking back from a psychological distance—with the partially distorted view that hindsight gives. Unlike any other account I know of, this one was put down in process, while the persons reaching for reality were praying for light, that is, before they actually crossed the threshold and entered.

So it meets the seeker of truth, not from afar, but on his own turf, and walks beside him, as far as he will go, on the road to Rome. The difficulties encountered, especially by Protestants, are clearly experienced, faced, and worked through. The claims of the Church Christ founded are presented, I think, lucidly, relying on the wisdom of Dryden's couplet: "Truth has such a face and such a mien/ As to be loved needs only to be seen."

What you have in your hands is an existential, but rational, book, written before the author and his family were received into the Church. Another out-of-the-ordinary facet: both husband and wife were mainline Protestant ministers.

So what happened to them after their destiny decision? As you might expect, some of their teachers, friends, and family warned against the foolhardy move. "Why not be an Episcopalian?" some advised. "You'd have everything but the pope. And, after all, who needs *him*?'' What but pride, or some hidden need, could seduce anyone into accepting an outmoded, medieval superstition? After three years at Yale Divinity School and a summer at Union Theological Seminary—studying under such greats as Roland Bainton, Paul Tillich, Richard and Reinhold Niebuhr—why had they opted for a hand-me-down, ready-made package? Why had they given up thinking for themselves?

Their parents, unselfish Protestants who lived for their children, gave them full, if somewhat uncomprehending, support in more ways than one. So they wandered off into the unknown wilderness, trusting heaven for desert rain. On principle no job had been arranged in advance. I'd been a reporter for newspapers in New Haven and New York, a minister for churches in Maine and Connecticut. At Bethlehem Steel I'd worked as a day laborer, shoveling dirt, wearing hip boots to clean out acid pits. I ended up teaching in a college, but not till many months later.

Meanwhile, two 33-year-old mendicants lived on the hospitality of Regina Laudis Monastery, whose Mother Benedict instructed them in the faith, and with their parents in Ohio and Pennsylvania. These nomads were accompanied by their daughters, gypsy beggars ages two and three, who were sometimes allowed, as their parents were not, behind the high monastery walls. There, I suppose, with the other sisters they said prayers for the Holy Father and the peace of the world. But, as it turned out, they did not have early vocations.

The New World

Back into the world they went, rejected by clock and cloister. And what a pregnant world it was! Ms. Liberty, or rather Ms. License, was slouching toward the sexual revolution of the 1960s. A virulent, global pantheism, intolerant of the moral absolutes of divine revelation, was gathering strength. America was about to enter the "I have my truth, you have your truth, and anyway, truth doesn't matter" era. In bedrooms, ballrooms, and brokerage offices hedonistic greed was gearing up "with all wicked deception" (2 Thess. 2:10). In cafeterias, classrooms, and yes, churches, reaction was growing against Christian principles and eternal values. Cultural institutions—arts, media, universities, foundations—were infiltrated by the pervasive forces of re-emerging modernism, which exalted individual experience over transcendent truth.

In the Catholic Church those who espoused this immanentism, this "synthesis of all heresies," as it was called by Pope St. Pius X, sought to eviscerate the supernatural meaning of dogmatic formulas, aided by their subjective misinterpretations of the Second Vatican Council. In the wider world such "charitable" shadings of the faith were applauded.

Playing against this backdrop, the Supreme Court abolished prayer and Bible reading from the public schools and eventually much of public life. The Ten Commandments have been taken down from many court room walls. Unjust laws have been enacted, even a murderous one in *Roe vs. Wade.* The nation's morality and S.A.T. scores have gone down ever since, as many poor fathers disappear and family structures decompose. And being an indistinguishable part of the scene, millions of Catholics "in good conscience" went blindly along with it all. It makes you wonder to what extent their consciences and ours have actually been formed by the authentic teachings of the Church on faith and morals.

Now, like everyone else, our attitudes and choices are to a great extent controlled by the spirit of the age, which is aptly summed up in Iago's refrain, "Put money in thy purse." Increasing numbers of irresponsibles will not accept any limit on personal behavior. Moral turpitude in high places, reckless abuse of political power, have increased. The Ten Commandments have become the Ten Suggestions. We harken and salivate to the merchants of the media, who assure us that the more we have, the happier we'll be . . . so long as we don't let too many babies crowd in on our time here. We Catholics in the northeast continue to prove ourselves "good Americans" by sending pro-abortion co-religionists to Congress, where they vote to kill more unborn, even mostly born, babies. In some ways we don't measure up very well to the high moral teachings of the one true faith we profess.

But, dear non-Catholic reader, if you hesitate to consider seriously the claims of this Church, or if you are hesitating to enter it because some of its members seem hypocritical, come right in: there's always room for one more. Get aboard. St. Peter's Ship sails this day for heaven with a motley crew of sinners . . . like you and me.

In the past forty-five years, our lifetime in the Catholic Church, pulpit fare has grown comfortably silent about the danger of hell, Mass attendance has dropped at least a third, half belief has doubled, confessions have tithed. Troublesome numbers, wouldn't you say? As for the statistics on death, physical not spiritual, they're quite reliable commented Mark Twain: "One out of one dies."

"Dear God, what then?"

"Believe in the Lord Jesus, and you will be saved, you and your household" (Acts 16:31). My grace will see you through to life everlasting.

"But Lord, how do we get there from here in one piece? If I am going on a long last journey, how shall I prepare for it in advance?"

"I have sent my only Son to tell you. Listen to him."

Since entering the Yale Divinity School in 1945, we have tried to hear and follow him. But the people who claimed to represent him said so many different things. It was hard to know exactly where to hear his voice . . . until at last we realized that he had told us where.

What we did not realize was that the beliefs of the liberal Protestantism we were leaving—which increasingly accommodated its outlook to changing fashions of the dominant, secular culture— would invade the Catholic Church with a vengeance over the next four decades.

Thank God for the worldwide majority of loyal, reliable bishops. Thank heaven the Church's Founder entrusted its future to the successors of the apostles, who in our own day have produced the new *Catechism of the Catholic Church*. Every age has its one-eyed merchants of erroneous doctrine, and ours is no exception. These have made the *Catechism* their bête noir. They downplay or dilute it, misrepresent and undermine it, in a variety of subtle ways. Why do they dislike this God-given standard of authentic faith? Because it asserts definite truths, expecting Catholics to believe and follow what the Church, like its Founder, teaches with authority (Mark 1:22), since only by doing so can souls successfully weather the storms of life and make port.

Not as the Scribes

Those who reject this authority have a right as free individuals to do so. But they do not then follow revealed truth as the Roman Catholic Church has understood it down the ages. Since she has been guided by the Holy Spirit (John 16:13), avoiding both an indifferent syncretism and a false exclusivism, her essential teachings are not negotiable. For members of that Church even limited and occasional dissent is an illegitimate playing with fire and loss of faith. As Cardinal Newman put it in *A Grammar of Assent*, "There is no medium between assenting and not assenting." Charitable dialogue with sincere dissenters can sometimes be productive for both parties, but hardly on a relativistic basis that does not care what is true or false. Sincerity in error, however sincere, does not change reality, cannot undo what is. And, of course, the Church founded by Christ cannot accept, nor treat as equal, any alternative magisterium within her body, which is the Mystical Body of Christ.

When these polarizing questions arise, I would like to be more conciliatory toward some of the well-intentioned dissenters I know. But sitting on the fence hurts, and it produces bad results for souls. So friends, if you refuse to follow St. Peter and his successors, how can those of us who do accompany you? The perceptive Peter Kreeft comments: "Truth is always a better friend than someone who cannot endure its company." I must say reluctantly that we should be on our guard against those who claim to speak for Christ but contradict his Church. Those who teach what they please, or what pleases other people than our Lord and the magisterial authority he established, are they not—from the viewpoint of divine revelation—misguided, misdirecting leaders? They gamble with the eternal salvation of their followers. Some of them buy unwittingly into the diabolical side of the cosmic conflict. The false charts and false reckonings they sell will not take the buyers' ships to port.

There is only one set of charts and reckonings that does that dependably, only one seaworthy vessel that makes that last journey safely. And God, it seems, was calling us into St. Peter's Ship, the ark of saving truth, while many of its dissenting sailors and passengers were preparing a mutiny or slipping over the side at night.

So where did the voyage take us? In leaving vocations long prepared for, sailing away from the land we knew, were we recklessly risking our children's futures? "Do not be afraid," the angel of the One he served told St. Paul, "God has granted you all those who sail with you. So take heart" (Acts 27:24–25). We hoped that message applied to us, too.

Decades have passed, and now in the year 2000 we are walking the narrow way of our eightieth year. So far the grandchildren add up to seven boys and three girls. Our six children, ages 38 to 49, are all married to good and reliable mates . . . except for Father John, who came to the altar another way.

Marjorie, the better three-quarters, her traveler's day from glory to glory bent, has written in the souls of family and parish from the Christian Family Movement of the 1950s to her present chair of the local Evangelization 2000 committee. She has been a Parish Council member, Lector, and Minister of the Eucharist, through a long series of effective pastors and associate priests. For many years she taught the early grades in a public school to help pay the bills. Six children with well over a dozen college degrees didn't come cheap, in spite of scholarships and government loans.

In the Underwood line of Marjorie's family there have been Protestant ministers since before the Revolutionary War—from

Puritan Massachusetts to the Western Reserve of northern Ohio. Her roommates in college, Oberlin '45, called her with accurate connotation "Angel." She's a saintly person, an active part of the answer, the warm heart of the family.

Golden Days

Since we entered the sheepfold of the Roman Shepherd— Father, Mother, two young ladies—those four through birth and marital acquisition have become twenty-three. All of us got together Christmas 1995 in Boca Raton, Florida, to celebrate our Golden Wedding Anniversary. We were married by Rev. Roland Bainton March 21, 1946, in Marquand Chapel at the Yale Divinity School, where later we were jointly ordained to the ministry of the Congregational Church on June 24, 1951.

So far the marriage has lasted 54 years, as have many of the Christian beliefs Dr. Bainton and the other greats at YDS implanted. Overall, they did an admirable job of teaching and launching young Protestant ministers. They just didn't see the whole picture, and the pictures they did see were—from the Catholic viewpoint— individually distorted. Their differing interpretations of essential doctrine relativized the truth, and ecumenical progress, however desirable, can never be accomplished at the expense of revealed truth.

God's gifts to us of faith and family have been ongoing and expanding. Not exactly the progeny of Abraham, but a start, as suggested at the end of Chapter 10 above: "Manifold more in this present time" and, we hope for all our twenty-three *and for you*, "in the world to come life everlasting."

Realizing that last promise, the ultimate desire of the human heart, depends not only on God's amazing generosity, but also on our recognizing the reality of our situation and reacting vigorously. In a word, it depends on faith, an accepting response to God's revelation. St. Paul tells us: "Faith comes from what is heard, and what is heard comes by the preaching of Christ" (Rom. 10:17). Without it all else in the end is poison in the ear. Until we become accurately aware of our full context, its problem and answer, how can we respond appropriately? Until we realize that, independent of our limited human minds, there is such a thing as objective truth, we wander through shadowlands of uncertainty. Revealed truth puts us in contact with what is, seen and unseen, and if we seek it prayerfully, primarily, persistently, with its Author and the Divine Society he founded for our benefit. Trials, tribulations and sacrifices may follow, but the Lord never promised any of us a free ride.

So where were we going? Where was the unpredictable Deity taking us? We didn't have an inkling of his scenario for the next forty-five years. We knew that he planned to weave us into his hidden tapestry, but how? We tried to make our lives available. We prayed. We worked. We waited . . . without an iota of suspicion in those early days that his leadings, when they came, would direct us to cross an abyss.

Until my second year at YDS I didn't really know who Jesus Christ was and is. What was I to make of this man who claimed equality with God? Was he a liar, a lunatic, or what he claimed to be, God Incarnate? I was uncertain about those humanly impossible miracles. He calmed the storm, healed the sick, gave sight to the blind, raised the dead. Who could do that but the God who made them all to begin with? I failed to understand that Christ—crucified, risen from his tomb, ascended into heaven—was praying for us to the Father, planning the strange course of our conversion and beyond. He had become what we are so that we might become what he is. And he told us what to do about it: "Repent and believe the good news" . . . all of it, leaving nothing out. Once we become his willing listeners and penitent followers, Jesus forgives our sins and takes the lead in our lives. With his saints and angels he accompanies us through all the joys and tribulations along the way.

Travelers All

What delightful traveling companions he has sent our family over the past four decades!

First of all, that entertaining, peregrinating prince of apostles, Frank Sheed, paragon of apologists, crowd-collecting stump speaker from Hyde Park in London to Forty-second Street in New York, who visited our home regularly and answered our ongoing questions wisely. He was full of useful advice: "If you want to speak clearly, be sure you sound the last letter of every word."

A brilliant teacher, witty and charming, Frank was a memorable phrase-maker and an adroit handler of hecklers' taunts. Orthodox though he was, he called his shots as he saw them. Fr. Benedict Groeschel, C.F.R., remembers him saying, "Many Catholics have misplaced their confidence, putting it in the hierarchy instead of Christ. I am an expert on bad popes and the ugly side of the hierarchy, but I am a very happy Catholic. There is nothing a pope or bishop could say or do that would make me leave the Church, although there is a lot they could say or do that would make me want *them* to leave the Church."

Frank and his noble wife, Maisie Ward, our godparents when we entered the Church, founded the Catholic Evidence Guild and compiled its magnificent handbook, *Catholic Evidence Training Outlines*, a classic guide to understanding and explaining the truths of the Church.

However, nowhere in its clarifying pages does it divulge two little-known secrets I will now tell you about Frank. He once confided to us that he really wanted to be a song-and-dance man. Growing up in Australia with a Communist father and a Catholic mother, that was his first real longing in life. His later ambition was this: depending on what Christ had done for him, he hoped happily to enter into Purgatory, where the forgiven sinner is readied for the All Holy Presence (1 Cor. 3:12–15). The idea of a ticket straight to heaven troubled him. He felt he wasn't ready.

No twentieth century layman has done more to leaven and enliven the English-speaking Church than Frank Sheed. And he put into your hands the book you now hold.

More such would be needed to thank all our family's bene-factors. Our first priest adviser was a savvy son of Brooklyn, No Nonsense McSorley, Joseph, C.S.P., U.S. Army Chaplain in World War I, Master of Novices, Professor of Dogmatic Theology. He wasn't born yesterday. Actually, he was born in 1874, three years before my father. He warned us sagely: "Converts! Before you get done with 'born' Catholics, you'll eat a peck of dirt. But don't worry, the Lord will look after you." He has looked after us, in one way, through our family's wise spiritual director, Fr. James Halligan, who serves in New York's first Catholic parish, St. Peter's in lower Manhattan.

Our children grew up spending their weekends among the priests and sisters at Maryknoll, near Ossining, New York. Mothers General Mary Columba and Mary Coleman, Fathers John McConnell and John Considine, have since died holy deaths, and Bill McNaughton of the 10 May 1954 entry has been Bishop of Inchon, Korea, since August 24, 1961, daughter Catherine's fifth birthday . . . whom he married along with sisters Mary and Clare.

We are all included in the missionary outreach that Bishop McNaughton so well represents. "The Church exists in order to evangelize," according to the present Holy Father. Every priest and every member of the laity is by nature and vocation a missionary, within the parish and abroad. When the Holy Spirit opens a door of receptivity, we should bear an appropriate witness. The grace of God comes *to* us in order to come *through* us.

Working as an assistant to Bishop Fulton Sheen at the National Office of the Propagation of the Faith was another blessing God gave us. He was a star of the mid-century airways, a lightning rod for those who hated the Church but loved him.

Under his guidance the S.P.O.F. raised millions for the missions every year. I remember the dedicated people, the publication deadlines, his three o'clock rosary talks, and a particular incident. At age eight or nine, fourth daughter Clare accompanied us to the Tuesday night telecast studio. When she met His Excellency in his flowing robes, looking like an Arabian prince, she said to him wide-eyed: "You're beautiful!" He took her aside for a conference. She came back carrying a big new bill he had ceremoniously unpeeled from a roll in his pocket. Inspired, she went on through McGill, St. Andrews, and Tufts to become at twenty-three the youngest Director of Religious Education in Massachusetts, before marriage and children.

The other sisters are a landscape designer, an ophthalmology nurse, and Mary, the ballet historian and teacher who danced at the Met, the Hanover Opera & Ballet in Germany, and around Europe in a company with Nureyev. And they're each raising a family. The two boys we brought up with the help of four assistant mothers are now a priest and a commercial real estate specialist working for REIT in Boston. As children, the younger five were kept nicely in line by their loving, oldest sister, Margaret—whose landscape gardens on Fisher Island and Nantucket are as beautiful as herself.

For many years we have benefited from our family's friendship with Fathers Benedict Groeschel, C.F.R., and Avery Dulles, S.J., both most effective servants of the Lord. Our boys sequentially kept Fr. Benedict's accounts (not the higher kind) at Trinity Retreat, and Fr. Avery was our priest son's spiritual director at the Theological College of Catholic University in Washington, D.C.

We can never forget those angelic nuns of many orders. One of them was my boss when I taught European history at Manhattanville College, Sr. Kathryn Sullivan, R.S.C.J. Imagine being supervised by someone who often substituted for biblical and theological professors in Rome's seminaries. Sr. Kathryn has been a faithful friend and correspondent. As, indeed, has Sr. Mary Peter, O.P., former prioress of a couple dozen Irish Dominicans hidden a mile outside of Fatima in Monastery Pius XII. Such cloistered nuns are some of the happiest, because holiest, people on earth.

Family Friends

As you realize by now, this is a family book in its ramifications. God had to start somewhere, probably at the lowest point, but in the end he brought a whole family into the Church Christ founded. Which brings to mind the clergyman whose congregation gave him a medal for humility, but had to take it back because he kept wearing it in the pulpit. Families will humble you, knowing your weak points, and, as any priest can tell you, so will parishioners, who sometimes go home after a poor homily and have roast priest for Sunday dinner.

That is a no-no. Even a priest who *should* be roasted is a stand-in for Christ, who said: "He who hears you hears me, and he who rejects you rejects me, and he who rejects me rejects him who sent me" (Luke 10:16). As such, he should be reverenced, loved, honored, and, above all, prayed for. Any older priest can tell you that when he walked down the street in his younger days, passers-by would smile and say, "Hello, Father. Have a good day, Father." No more. Even some good Catholics may have forgotten that Fathers are spiritual fathers of Christ's family.

It is the family that the faith recognizes as the basic cell of society, while calling for individual conversion. The individual finds fulfillment in his own family, in the larger family of mankind, and, above all, in the Trinitarian family of God. As Christians and as human beings, we already belong to one family, even if we don't always behave well toward the other members.

Two members of our family, Margaret and Mary, both mentioned here and there in the 1954 entries, were born while we were still Protestant ministers. The others entered a Catholic home barely able to afford them. Catherine—a dedicated nurse, mother, and churchwoman in St. Louis, which city the Pope recently visited—came the same year this book was first published, Clare two years later. When Father John was born, 20 September 1960, on the 42nd anniversary of the day Padre Pio received the visible stigmata, we sent a family picture to that Capuchin monk of the 16 September 1954 entry.

Maria Pyle, an American Protestant convert who spent her life as Padre Pio's secretary, replied in late 1960: "Padre Pio held this picture at length in his precious hands and blessed the whole family and accepted all as his spiritual children. He repeated more than once, 'Mother, father, and six children.' Where is the sixth?"

There were only five children in the photo, so eventually I wrote back, rather brazenly by hindsight, "Can't he count?"

The reply was dated June 14, 1961:

> Dear friends, I can assure you Padre Pio did not speak of number *six* by mistake, and every word of his has a significance. He wants the decision as to the number to be left to God and with confidence and faith we must follow God's will! We thank you for your Mass offering which I consigned as soon as I received it—so probably the Mass has already been celebrated. If not, it will be soon, and Padre Pio continues to pray for you and your family.

Evidently we did leave it to God, because our second son, William Michael, was born October 13, 1962, forty-five years to the day after the miracle of the sun at Fatima.

Maria Pyle wrote again:

> Deo gratias! Your lovely photo of the family has been blessed by Padre Pio and he gladly accepts all as his spiritual children. He expects you to continue in all the good you are doing and to do still more and for the children just to be good. I can assure you that Padre Pio has been praying for you since your letter of 1953.

Padre Pio urged that our prayers be insistent, especially amid discouraging difficulties. The trials the Lord sends, he said, are all "signs of Divine love, jewels for the soul." Like St. Francis of Assisi, St. Catherine of Siena, and other focused saints, the now Blessed Pio—beatified in St. Peter's Square by His Holiness, Pope John Paul II, Sunday, May 2, 1999—evidenced a complete loyalty to St. Peter and his successors. He knew that those who knowingly reject the voice of Christ transmitted through the reliable teaching voice of his Church—which can be either the pope speaking with authority to the bishops of the world or his interpreting with authority their collegial consensus—are left with nothing but their own likes and preferences. How happily he would have received John Paul II's new *Catechism*! But he never in all his miraculous life prayed to the pope in Rome. Nor has any saint in the last two millennia.

Christus Solus est Omnia

Pope John Paul II summarizes the message of this book in thirteen words: "Jesus Christ is the answer to which every human life is the question." No one can substitute for Jesus himself, not even his mother, though she is closer to him than any other created being and participates in all that he is doing for us. God Incarnate came here with her consent and through her body. According to his will, she who gave us the source of all grace co-operates in its distribution. Her intercessory care for each of us is one of God's greatest gifts.

The saints and angels in heaven are a cloud of faithful witnesses all pointing to that unexpected hidden treasure for which the truly worldly-wise will sell all (Matt. 13:44). They summon us to him who is the Savior of our souls, the reason for everything, the riches of eternity. They sing in harmony: "We adore you, O Christ, and we praise you, because by your holy cross you have redeemed the world."

In his *Letter to the Colossians* (1:27) St. Paul tells us the answer to all our needs: "The secret is this, Christ in you, your hope of glory." Loving Jesus above all is the way to heaven. The deepest intimacy of our souls, our very identity must belong to him. Where else should a Christian find his autobiographical center? "My Me is God," said St. Catherine of Genoa, "nor do I recognize any other Me except my God himself."

This is not a mere metaphor but a spiritual reality. In fact, all three Persons of the Blessed Trinity indwell the soul in a state of grace, doing the work of salvation from within its deepest recesses.

But even this gift is exceeded by our Lord's Eucharistic Presence, the daily miracle that nourishes his continued indwelling. "He who eats my flesh and drinks my blood abides in me, and I in him" (John 6:56). Christ is really and substantially present—Body and Blood, Soul and Divinity—in the consecrated bread and wine, which are now physically Christ and no longer bread and wine except in appearance. The host is the Lord himself. What is needed in the Church today, perhaps more than anything else, is a fuller teaching of this mystery to the faithful and a widespread return of genuine devotion to Jesus Christ in the Eucharist.

The *Catechism of the Catholic Church* describes all seven sacraments as " 'powers that comes forth' from the Body of Christ, which is ever-living and life-giving. They are actions of the Holy Spirit at work in his Body, the Church" (1116). It tells us that the Eucharist is "the source and summit of the Christian life" (1324). This miraculous mystery is central to the divine economy and leads, if we allow, to the beatific vision.

Here on this third planet from the sun we exiles from Eden are always *in via*, on the way of choice to one of two final destinations. Welcome him, and God goes with us on our journey. As Moses told his wandering people: "and in the wilderness, where you have seen how the LORD your God bore you, as a man bears his son, in all the way that you went until you came to this place" (Dt. 1:31).

He carries us and our burdens of guilt and mortality—from without by his Providence, from within by his Presence. Communion with this inner Divine Guest, who is ever about the business of transforming us into his Being, is the essential element of the Christian life. In the end, the saints tell us, total surrender to God leaves nothing behind of self-will. When all is at his disposal, he acts in us and through us to carry out in our own day his eternal plan and promise (John 6:40).

When does this effective indwelling begin? At baptism, which is the basis of our Christian life. St. Gregory of Naziansus calls the first sacrament: "God's most beautiful and magnificent gift." Let me share with you such an event: in this case it produced a priest. The following letter is dated June 7, 1977, when the boy mentioned was sixteen. He had just written an essay titled, "John Neumann: First Male Saint For U.S." "My dear Oliver," it begins, "I thank God that your son, John, whom I baptized, has responded to the infusion of the Holy Spirit in his soul by following your footsteps and becoming interested in a saint. He writes well and gives promise of a beautiful future for God and the Church." The letter ends, "With prayers and blessings, I am, Faithfully yours in Christ, + Fulton Sheen."

Now in heaven the instrument of that infusion—who daily spent an early morning hour on his knees before the Blessed Sacrament, a vow he made at ordination—is still aiding his charge with follow-up prayers, we like to think. Twenty-three Junes after that letter, Father John has completed three years of study in Rome, earning his licentiate in Canon Law and doctorate in theology. He graduated summa cum laude with a doctoral dissertation titled: "Jean-Jacques Olier's Priestly Spirituality: Mental Prayer and Virtue as the Foundation for the Direction of Souls." Now serving as Chancellor of a diocese, at 39 Msgr. Barres is already a true *alter Christus* and a fine Father of souls.

I think, deep down, what I personally wanted in this life, other than God himself, was to be a good father. To be that, or a good mother, you'd have to be a saint. But we sinners keep trying. We know that the primary job of good parents is to help their children keep the faith and get to heaven. Relying on divine aid, we try to incarnate in our own and our children's lives two words: *God first*, his honor and glory, nothing else in his place. This is simply a recognition of reality: how can supposedly sane human beings attempt to relegate to the background Someone who is All-Power? Our plan and purpose is clear: one will—Christ's, one goal—the Father's glory. Compared to these, things of earth dwindle in importance. Consider Fr. Olier's comment about the really big money: "All the riches of the earth are but rags compared to the glory of God."

As Catholic parents, we have the duty and opportunity of passing on to our children the motivating spark in our lives. It can be

put into nine words: "Jesus, my God, I love you above all things."
We pray that "they in turn will tell their children" (Ps. 78:3–7),
thus bequeathing spiritual wealth from generation to generation.
As assistant creators, we are also evangelizers who communicate
God's love, helping him distribute his bounty of eternal hope—
now and far into the future.

As for this ephemeral book, if it has shed any light on your
path, let it be like the Star of Bethlehem, which led the Magi to
the Christ Child, then disappeared. There is no gift I have offered
you in these pages which does not pale and disappear in *his* light
. . . but perhaps, unexpectedly, in answer to *your* prayer and out
of compassion for *your* need, somehow he will shine through a
page or a paragraph into your mind and heart.

God created you to make you eternally happy. Before the world
began he knew you to the marrow of your bones and mapped out
the path of your life. No one else can give him what he seeks from
you. What is that? John Paul II tells us in his inspiring "Letter
to Artists" (Easter Sunday, 1999): "All men and women are entrusted with the task of crafting their own life: in a certain sense,
they are to make of it a work of art, a masterpiece" . . . with
God's help. As a child of his love, you can expect this help, his
special care, in the regular routine of your life and in many un-
foreseen ways. The divine spark within you—which calls your
whole being to the good, the true, and the beautiful in God—
has been given you to share with others in spiritual and physical
need. "Each soul is my favorite," he told Gabrielle Bossis in *He
and I.* "I choose some only to reach the others."

We dare not neglect his call, however it comes. The music of
a man or a woman's life grows dangerously discordant unless the
player knows his chords and keys: there is but One who does.
We do well only if we let him play our song. In doing so he will
play *his* song through us.

Last of all, may I offer to the Holy Spirit and to you a song
in praise of his spouse, the Blessed Virgin Mary, who cooperates
in bringing her Son to birth in our souls, that we may say with

St. Paul: "it is no longer I who live, but Christ who lives in me" (Gal. 2:20).

This song was given to a very minor troubadour of God somewhere in the secular night of the early nineties. I have found that the flow of its echoing music and changing imagery is healing and opens spiritual gates. Through it, I hope, the mysterious Lady it celebrates, Mother of Our Lord and Mother of us all, will give you joy and sing to you in the dark hours of the night.

The Mystery of Mary

You saw the windstorm flames descend,
Fishermen moving inland to mend
The hopes of men with heaven to hear;
Now we embark on ground swells of fear;
      We sail to water's end:
      O Star of the Sea, be near,
Shining guardian, guiding friend.

Lead us by fire through trackless night;
Release our eyes from shadowed sight:
Maid, who can make—from little—all
And fructify the barren fall
      With prayer from heaven's height,
      To you in hope we call,
O Mother of the Lord of light.

Treasure room, where the Spirit King
Has hid a brilliant, priceless thing;
Celestial mine, producing gold
That gives true value to the mold
      Of time: Sweet Mary, sing,
      And let God's poor be told
Of aid good men and angels bring.

Your spark of pulsing glory grew
To warm this wintry world anew;
You set the Morning Star in place
From out of Jacob's darkened race

And pondered visions through
The light on Moses' face:
O Maid of grace, we look to you.

Through your transparency we gaze.
In awe at clouded heights, ablaze
With conversing splendor yet serene
In majesty; your glass is clean:
No interposing haze
But ours obscures the scene:
O loyal Queen, we join your praise.

For you are now what we would be,
Eternal flesh by heaven's decree;
Whose earthly mien, so chaste and fair,
Still trembles on the Maytime air:
O Virgin, lead us free
From sin and hell's despair;
In lands of unlikeness let us see.

Show us the Child of dawn, we pray,
As Simeon saw your piercing day
And hailed the life-restoring sun;
And if some healing work begun
Too late should meet delay,
O Mother, let it run
On feet of resurrected clay.

Surely your Son will not deny
The prayer you offer with our cry
Of need, whose blood in oneness beat
From Nazareth to the doleful street
That led to a sunless sky:
God's refuge and retreat,
Be with us now and when we die.

Abyss of love, conceiving night,
Where none can fathom depth or height:
Exalted lowliness, the bride
Of Him who rules the timeless tide
    Of seas beyond our sight:
    O Virgin, be our guide
Till we have reached the lands of light.

Notes

1. This journal was begun on our eighth wedding anniversary.

2. Throughout Part One friends and some lecturers are listed by initials only, though full names are used in crediting quotations from books.

3. Arnold Lunn, *Now I See* (New York, Sheed and Ward, 1945), p. 256.

4. Ronald Knox, *Enthusiasm* (New York, Oxford, 1950), p. 423.

5. Joseph Fuchs, "Situation Ethics and Theology," *Theology Digest*, Winter 1954, p. 28.

6. C. C. Morrison, "Eclipse of the Ecumenical Goal," *Christian Century*, January 13, 1954, pp. 42–44.

7. For an appreciation of Kierkegaard and a stricture on Sartre by the author see *Saturday Review of Literature*, May 31, 1947, p. 14.

8. For a perceptive analysis of the disparity between liberal Protestant emphasis on human effort and Catholic emphasis on supernatural grace see Rosalind Murray, *The Further Journey* (New York, McKay, 1952).

9. *Advance*, May 31, 1954, p. 22.

10. *National Catholic Almanac*, 1952 (Paterson, N.J., St. Anthony's Guild), p. 268.

11. *Advance Reports* (New York, General Council of the Congregational Christian Churches, 1954), pp. 47, 153.

12. Eugenio Zolli, *Before the Dawn* (New York, Sheed and Ward, 1954), p. 80.

13. René Fulop-Miller, *The Saints that Moved the World* (New York, Crowell, 1945), p. 50.

14. Hilaire Belloc, *The Great Heresies* (New York, Sheed and Ward, 1938), p. 172.

15. C. C. Morrison, *Christian Century*, June 2, 1954, pp. 666–668.

16. *Ibid.*, p. 668.

17. *Kirkridge Contour* (Bangor, Pennsylvania, April 1954), no. 76.

18. "It is my personal opinion that the Anglo-Catholics, with the exception of those few who simply accept everything that the Roman Catholics do, including their method of theologizing, are anxious to *use* the consecrated formulas of the abiding Church, but give them a meaning foreign to their genuine intent in order to harmonize the Catholic propositions with the contemporary moods and movements. As a result, Anglo-Catholic theology is the only true Center theology in Protestantism, but it is also an elegant instance of 'double talk' whereby the speaker can be understood simultaneously both as a Catholic and as a naturalist. There is no insincerity in this position, but there is a voluntary ambiguity deriving from an indeliberate theological schizophrenia." Gustave Weigel, S.J., *A Survey of Protestant Theology in Our Day* (Westminster, Md., Newman Press, 1954), p. 28.

19. Leonard Cheshire, as quoted in *Time*, June 14, 1954, p. 72.

20. Martin Boegner, *Le Problème de l'Unité Chrétienne* (Paris 1947), p. 129.

21. E. E. Reynolds, *St. Thomas More* (New York, Kenedy, 1953), p. 291.

22. *Ibid.*, p. 293.

23. *Ibid.*, p. 359.

24. Howard Brinton, "Asia and Scientific Materialism," *Christian Century*, June 9, 1954, p. 703. Not all Quakers are neutral-pacifist on this issue of Communism. Even those who are may help to provide a balance against the professional anti-Communist rabble rousers who would ride this national obsession of ours into power. Will those who have thus sought to "fan and exploit this neurotic obsession" be held guiltless when judgment is made of its ultimate effect upon the characters of our children, who are the future America?

25. E. McLaughlin, *People's Padre* (Boston, Beacon, 1954), p. 133.

26. *Ibid.*, p. 140.

27. *Ibid.*, p. 122.

28. *New Haven Journal-Courier*, June 25, 1954, p. 4.

29. As listed in A *Study by the Committee on Free Church Polity and Unity* (June 1954), the nine forms are as follows: Purely Cooperative Efforts, Councils of Churches, Federated Relationships, Covenanted Relationships, The "University Plan," Federal Union, Plurality, Complete Organic Union, and Union With The Roman Catholic Church.

30. *Ibid.*, p. 80.

31. *Ibid.*, p. 81.

32. "By liberalism I mean the anti-dogmatic principle and its developments. . . . Liberalism then is the mistake of subjecting to human judgment those revealed doctrines which are in their nature beyond and independent of it, and of claiming to determine on intrinsic grounds the truth and value of propositions which rest for their reception simply on the external authority of the Divine Word." John Henry Newman, *Apologia Pro Vita Sua* (New York, Sheed and Ward, 1946), pp. 32, 192. The term liberalism as used by Leo XIII refers to "the attitude of those men who refuse to submit their wills to any law prescribed by a higher authority than their own, and quite especially, by the authority of God. Reduced to its very essence, liberalism is the rejection of any divine and supernatural law." Etienne Gilson, *The Church Speaks to the Modern World: The Social Teachings of Leo XIII* (New York, Image, 1954), Introduction, p. 8.

33. Sir Frederic Kenyon, *The Reading of the Bible* (London, J. Murray and Transatlantic Arts, 1944), p. 91.

34. *The Congregationalists* (St. Paul, Radio Replies Press, 1948), p. 25.

35. Visser 't Hooft, "What Will the Evanston Assembly Say?", *Advance*, February 22, 1954, p. 22.

36. *St. Thérèse of Lisieux, the Little Flower of Jesus*, ed. by T. N. Taylor (New York, Kenedy, 1926).

37. Sigrid Undset, *St. Catherine of Siena* (New York, Sheed and Ward, 1954), p. 92.

38. *New York Herald Tribune*, August 4, 1954, p. 16.

39. "Ask Us Another" column, *Our Sunday Visitor*, August 1, 1954.

40. *Chicago Sunday Tribune*, August 15, 1954, p. 1.

41. *Poems from Italy* (Printed in the Field by No. 5 Mobile Printing Section, C.M.F., 1944), p. 5. The chief change is in the fourth line which formerly read: "And force submission to his just demand."

42. Sigrid Undset, *op. cit.*, pp. 182–195.

43. *Ibid.*, p. 186.

44. *Ibid.*, p. 187.

45. Ronald Knox, *A Spiritual Aeneid* (Westminster, Md., Newman Press, 1948), p. 202.

46. Martin Luther, *Unterricht von den Heiligen an die Kirche zu Erfurt* (1522), as quoted in Richard Baumann, *To See Peter* (New York, McKay, 1953), p. 13.

47. F. J. Sheed, *Theology and Sanity* (New York, Sheed and Ward, 1946), p. 247.

48. As quoted in B. L. Conway, *The Question Box* (New York, Paulist Press, 1929), pp. 368–369.

49. As quoted in J. A. McClorey, *The Inspiration of the Bible* (London, Herder, 1929), pp. 46–47.

50. "The commonest criticism is of the character of Catholics —of popes, bishops, priests and lay-people. People observe that this or that pope is immoral, this or that bishop is worldly, this or that priest is a bully or a snob or lazy, this or that layman is a corrupt politician or an unjust employer or a defaulting bookmaker or a scandalmonger. Catholics can be found in all these categories. But even if the proportion of unpleasing Catholics at every level were as great as the Church's severest critic thinks, the criterion would still be the wrong one . . . the main point is that it is through this strange assortment of human beings that Christ Our Lord gives the gifts of Truth and Life. No one who knows his own desperate need of those gifts would be kept at a distance by the character of the human means through which Christ has chosen that they shall have them, any more than a man hungry for

bread will be kept from it by doubts about the moral excellence of the baker. But if a man does not know about the gifts, he is bound to have strong views about the character of the purveyors, for the Catholic Church is a spectacular body and the vices of Catholics not likely to be overlooked." F. J. Sheed, *op. cit.*, p. 344.

51. "To go against conscience is neither right nor safe," Luther also told Eck at the Diet of Worms. "A single friar who goes counter to all Christianity for a thousand years must be wrong," replied the Emperor Charles. "He recognizes only the authority of Scripture, which he interprets in his own sense," charged the Edict of Worms.

My own belief is that Luther's conscience was sick and erroneous, though he seemed to follow it honestly every step of the road that led him away from Rome. As one of my thoughtful anti-Catholic friends is fond of saying: "The road to Rome is a two-way street." And so it is! On that highway seemingly honest travellers sometimes pass each other going in opposite directions.

May Almighty God, unto whom all hearts are open and all desires known, have mercy on us all!

52. Sigismondo Tizio, as quoted by K. Algermissen, *Christian Denominations* (St. Louis, Herder, 1946), p. 718.

53. Roland H. Bainton, *The Reformation of the Sixteenth Century* (Boston, Beacon, 1952), p. 24.

54. The following charitable Roman Catholic evaluation of Luther's character would lead us to believe that he might now be in heaven: "It is certain that Christianity's supernatural way of thought, the profound consciousness of sin, the yearning for redemption, and·the love of God never deserted Luther right down to the end of his life." K. Algermissen, *op. cit.*, p. 760.

55. Richard Baumann, *To See Peter* (New York, McKay, 1953), p. 9.

56. For a friendly Catholic study of Luther, the Reformation and the problem of reunion see Karl Adam's *One and Holy* (New York, Sheed and Ward, 1951).

57. See Hans Lilje, *Luther Now* (Philadelphia, Muhlenberg Press, 1952), p. 60.

58. Roland H. Bainton, *Here I Stand: A Life of Martin Luther* (New York, Abingdon-Cokesbury, 1950), p. 54.

59. C.B. Moss, *The Christian Faith* (London, S.P.C.K., 1943), p. 198.

60. See Chapter IX, "The Analyst and the Confessor," in Victor White, *God and the Unconscious* (Chicago, Regnery, 1953).

61. Martin Luther, trans. Theodore Graebner, *A Commentary on St. Paul's Epistle to the Galatians* (Grand Rapids, Zondervan, n.d.), pp. 76, 127.

62. E. E. Reynolds, *op. cit.*, p. 165.

63. E.g.—"In the beginning Congregationalists were actuated by certain principles in forming their view of the church. The first principle was anti-Romanism. The Congregationalists desired to strip from the Church of England all the 'rags of anti-Christ.' " Roland H. Bainton, "Is Congregationalism Sectarian?", *Christian Century*, February 24, 1954, p. 234.

64. As quoted in Hermann Rauschning, *The Voice of Destruction* (New York, Putnam, 1940), p. 54.

65. D.R. Davies, *The Sin of Our Age* (New York, Macmillan, 1947), p. 33.

66. Erich Adikes, *Kant's Opus Posthumum.*

67. A. N. Whitehead, *Religion in the Making* (New York, Macmillan, 1926), p. 90.

68. Fulton Sheen, *The Philosophy of Religion* (New York, Appleton-Century-Crofts, 1948), p. 206

69. Arnold Lunn, *op. cit.*, pp. 73 ff.

70. Ronald Knox, *Enthusiasm*, p. 37.

71. *Ibid.*, p. 163.

72. *Ibid.*, p. 135.

73. C. C. Martindale, *The Faith of the Roman Church* (New York, Sheed and Ward, 1951), pp. 111–112.

74. Martin Luther, 1524, as contained in the *Hymnal and Liturgies of the Moravian Church* (Bethlehem, Penna., Provincial Synod, 1920), p. 34.

75. Oscar Cullmann, *Peter* (Philadelphia, Westminster, 1953), p. 12.

76. *Ibid.*, pp. 235, 230.

77. *Ibid.*, p. 114.

78. L. Christiani, "Evacuations at the Vatican," *Theology Digest*, Winter 1954, p. 37.

79. "It is equally unwise to consider St. Paul's rebuke to Peter as evidence that Paul at least in no way recognized in Peter a superior (pp. 46 f.). The evidence may be read otherwise. Dr. T. G. Jalland, e.g., in *The Church and the Papacy* (pp. 60, 64), thinks that St. Paul's alarm at St. Peter's attitude is quite inexplicable unless underlying it there is a recognition of the unique and normative importance of any decision of St. Peter." J. F. McConnell, M.M., in his review of Cullmann's *Peter*, *Catholic Biblical Quarterly*, vol. xvi, no. 3 (July 1954), p. 365.

80. "And if a 'development' reaches a point at which it is officially taken up by the Church and built formally and finally into her structure, it must be a genuine development and not a corruption. This, of course, is not a matter of proof but of faith—faith in that unfailing purpose of Christ which the New Testament records in the words: 'The gates of hell shall not prevail' against Christ's Church." B. C. Butler, *The Church and Infallibility* (New York, Sheed and Ward, 1954), p. 124.

81. Trans. C. C. Richardson, *Early Christian Fathers* (Philadelphia, Westminster, 1953), pp. 73, 70.

82. *Ibid.*, p. 118.

83. *Ibid.*, p. 115.

84. Pope Leo XIII, *The Unity of the Church* (New York, Paulist Press, 1949), p. 28.

85. As quoted, *Ibid.*, pp. 28–29.

86. As quoted, *Ibid.*, p. 29.

87. W. R. Inge, *Christian Mysticism* (New York, Scribners, 1899,) pp. 329–330.

88. F. J. Sheed, *op. cit.*, p. 342.

89. See Ronald Knox, *A Spiritual Aeneid*, pp. 220–22.

90. Hilaire Belloc, *The Catholic Church and History* (New York, Macmillan, 1929), p. 59.

91. *Ibid.*, p. 82.

92. As quoted in *The Pope Is Infallible* (London, Catholic Truth Society, 1953), p. 16.

93. Arnold Lunn, *op. cit.*, p. 132.

94. Philip Hughes in his "honest-where-it-hurts" single volume masterpiece *A Popular History of the Catholic Church* (New York, Macmillan, 1953), p. 93, maintains that St. Gregory VII was forced into this position by the Emperor's plans for Church subjugation.

95. Thomas Sugrue, *A Catholic Speaks His Mind* (New York, Harper, 1951), p. 23.

96. Bishop Fulton Sheen's column, *Hartford Times*, July 10, 1954, p.5.

97. As quoted in J. L. Stoddard, *Rebuilding a Lost Faith* (New York, Kenedy, 1922), p. 168.

98. J. C. Macaulay, *The Heresies of Rome* (Chicago, Moody Press, 1946), p. 52.

99. As quoted in F. Mangan, *The Real Presence* (London, Catholic Truth Society, 1953), p. 16.

100. See end of Chapter 2, Part Two, this book.

101. Sigrid Undset, *op. cit.*, p. 136.

102. As quoted in B. L. Conway, *op. cit.*, p. 271.

103. J. P. Arendzen, *What Becomes of the Dead* (New York, Sheed and Ward, 1951), p. 63.

104. H. G. Graham, *Purgatory* (New York, Paulist Press, 1914), p. 8.

105. Sigrid Undset, *op. cit.*, p. 12.

106. Fulton Sheen, *The World's First Love* (New York, Garden City, 1952), p. 53.

107. As quoted in B. L. Conway, *op. cit.*, p. 353.

108. *Yes . . . the Mother of God Will Help You* (St. Louis, Knights of Columbus, 1951), p. 16. See the last chapter of this booklet, "The Mary Catholics Honor Is in the Bible," for a refutation of

Protestant misrepresentations of certain gospel references to Mary, such as supposed rebukes of her by her Son, etc.

109. As quoted in Lon Francis, *What Think Ye of Mary?* (Huntington, In., Our Sunday Visitor Press, 1954), p. 14. See this booklet for a refutation similar to the one mentioned under footnote 108.

110. As quoted in James McVann, *The Assumption* (New York, Paulist Press, 1950), p. 19.

111. As quoted in *Yes . . . the Mother of God, op. cit.,* pp. 30–31.

112. Jerome Hamer, O.P., "Mariology and Protestant Theology," *Theology Digest,* Spring 1954, pp. 67–70.

113. John Henry Newman, *The New Eve* (Oxford, Newman Bookshop, 1952), pp. 49–50.

114. John Beevers, *The Sun Her Mantle* (Westminster, Md., Newman Press, 1953), p. 15.

115. *Ibid.,* p. 43.

JHCS

37, 39, 42 43 (HOSPITAL...) 165
44 45 49 58, 59 60 177
62-3
74 76 78-9
81--? SEUSE)
86-87 HANORE
89-90 DEC 95-7 DECISION
!!! "CROSSING THE THRESHOLD"

+ 1. OB - ANNOUNCED FOR DIOCESE RVC
!!! 12/9/16
JHCS BDAY

CARDINAL NEWMAN
ST. JOHN NEWMAN ?